D1602338

Centre Parties

Polarization and Competition in European Parliamentary Democracies

Reuven Y. Hazan

PINTER

London and Washington

PINTER
A Cassell Imprint
Wellington House, 125 Strand, London WC2R 0BB
PO Box 605, Herndon, VA 20172

First published in 1997
© Reuven Y. Hazan 1997

British Library Cataloguing in Publication Data
A catalogue record for this book is available from the British Library.

ISBN 1–85567–431–9 (Hardback)

Library of Congress Cataloging-in-Publication Data
Hazan, Reuven Y., 1962–
    Centre parties: polarization and competition in European parliamentary democracies/ Reuven Y. Hazan.
        p. cm.
    Includes bibliographical references and index.
    ISBN 1–85567–431–9 (hardcover)
    1. Center parties – Europe.   2. Europe – Politics and government – 1945–   3. Democracy – Europe.   I. Title.
JN94.A979H39   1997
423.2'15'094 – dc20   96–43840
                                                                                                          CIP

Typeset by York House Typographic Ltd, London
Printed and bound in Great Britain by Biddles Limited, Guildford and King's Lynn

To Francine

Acknowledgements

I would like to thank Giovanni Sartori, Lewis Edinger, Douglas Chalmers, Robert Shapiro, David Lawrence, Donald Hancock and Herbert Kitschelt for reading drafts of this study, or particular chapters, and for providing advice, helpful comments, guidance and suggestions without which this research would have been much harder to complete.

Contents

List of Figures

List of Tables

Part I

The Context

1

Centre Parties, Party Systems, Electoral Competition and Government Stability

1.1   The Paradox of the Centre

What kind of impact do centre parties have? More precisely, what is the bearing of the existence and growth of centre parties on party system and government stability? If a multiparty system is faced with an onslaught of polarization, will the presence of centre parties abate this negative development, or enhance it? Will a growth in the electoral strength of the centre parties force the other parties – who are undergoing the process of polarization – to moderate their positions in order to court the centre, or will the growth of the centre push these parties further out and exacerbate polarization?

Reformist parties in the historical democracies of France and Britain, former agrarian parties in Scandinavia and new parties in the re-emergent democracies of Southern, Central and Eastern Europe have all adopted the propitious centre label, which has, for the most part, received favourable attention as a moderating factor. A centre party, so the assertion implies, can be a voter-exchange party, a resting place for voters discontented with one party but unable to swing to the opposite pole. The centre party can thus maintain the central orientation of the party system. According to this logic, centre parties restrain any impulse towards polarization. Moreover, if the party system is already experiencing a process of polarization, the existence of centre parties can serve as a point of attraction for voters who are dismayed by the ongoing radicalization.

An examination of contemporary centre parties may, however, prove the opposite. While the centre's moderating factors have received both theoretical mention and empirical praise, the opposite tendency of the centre to contribute to polarization has generally been ignored empiri-cally, and treated as if it were a lesser consequence theoretically. Indeed, centre parties may also thrive on and enhance polarization. Therefore, the growth of centre parties could prove to have an opposite effect than that of moderating the party system and thereby enhancing government stability.

But can a centre survive in the face of polarization? Will the divisive forces emanating from the two poles tear it apart? In a society split between two extreme political positions, centre parties might find it very difficult to succeed. In such a constellation the forces tearing society apart could attack the centre, ignore its call for moderation, and end up pulverizing it from both sides. However, it is precisely in this situation that a strong centre is most crucial. Will the centre then be crushed in a polarized party system, or will it attempt to feed off this trend and present itself as the only moderate influence that the voters can support? In other words, is it possible that centre parties thrive only in a society characterized by consensus – although it is in just such a society that a strong centre is both superfluous and irrelevant – or also in those societies undergoing polarization? Was Starzinger (1965: 16) correct when he stated that 'the center is least realistic where it is most relevant, and most realistic where it is least relevant'?

If the centre can also capitalize on, and maybe even beget, polariza-tion, then it is necessary to question the capacity of centre parties to moderate political polarization – for it is this essential moderating role that pervades much of the literature on the centre – and to reassess its limitations. The intuitive conceptualization of centre parties as a force of moderation could be incorrect. Herein lies the paradox of the centre. Yet most of the literature has ignored both the translation of reality into theory and the elaboration of an alternative, or counter-intuitive conceptualization. The paradox can be settled by answering one question: are centre parties related to party system polarization?

This study sets out to solve the paradox of the centre by ascertaining what kind of impact centre parties have in a multiparty system. It posits that *there is a relationship between the parliamentary strength of centre parties and the level of party system polarization*. Based on a systematic analysis of this hypothesized relationship, which verifies its existence and assesses its direction, two arguments, or theoretical explanations, are formu-lated which contribute to the refining of party systems theory. In the process, this research also focuses on the impact that centre parties have on party competition, because if centre parties gain from polariza-tion – rather than are destroyed by it – they might attempt to exacerbate this process. If this proves to be true, then the centre's intuitive moderating role becomes highly questionable.

This study is made up of four parts. Part I, The Context, has two chapters. This chapter presents the theoretical groundwork on how the centre is perceived in the literature, offering two opposing views. It concludes with a presentation of the research hypothesis, variables and agenda. Chapter 2 presents a definitional clarification of the centre – a term that has been stretched so far that it can no longer serve any analytical purpose. It also addresses such related terms as middle parties, pivotal parties, median parties, central parties and centre label parties in the process of divorcing them from the term centre parties.

Part II, The Model, is composed of four chapters. Chapter 3 analyses the empirical cross-national data on centre parties and party system polarization. It investigates the existence of a relationship between these two variables and assesses its direction. Chapter 4 raises two theoretical explanations for the relationship uncovered, and produces a model that elaborates this relationship. Chapters 5 and 6 empirically test both of the explanations elaborated in the model, in order to assess their validity.

Part III, Empirical Inquiry, is also made up of four chapters. Chapter 7 presents two case studies, chosen based on the findings of the cross-national analysis, and outlines their party systems. Chapter 8 elaborates core concepts in the two countries, using the terminology developed in this study. Chapters 9 and 10 use the two cases to assess which of the model's two theoretically elaborated and empirically validated explanations are supported by a more temporally comprehensive investigation within a country-specific context. The analysis verifies one of the two, and discards the other.

Part IV, Theoretical Implications, presents two concluding chapters. Chapter 11 returns to the theoretical arena and refines the model. It explicates the findings of this research, offers extensions and evaluates the impact of the centre's performance in regard to polarization. Chapter 12 applies this research's findings and their impact to party system theory, electoral competition and government stability.

1.2 Democratic Systems Typology and the Centre

The concern over democratic stability, one of the main aspects of comparative politics in general, has influenced party systems literature since its emergence in the post-war period. This focus produced an emphasis on the study of comparative governments, which in turn generated a dichotomous classification of democratic systems: stable versus unstable. Almond (1956), for example, described the difference between an Anglo-American type of political system based on a homogeneous political culture, which is associated with stability, and a Continental-European type with a fragmented political culture, which is conducive to instability.[1]

The dichotomous classification of democratic systems was reflected in the literature on party systems through the presumed dichotomy between democratically stable two-party systems and unstable multi-party systems. The concern over democratic stability thus pervaded the study of party systems by adopting the number of parties criterion to distinguish not only between the two types of stable versus unstable democracies in general, but also between stable versus unstable party systems in particular. Lipset (1959: 90), for example, clearly stated that 'two party systems are better than multi-party systems', because they are conducive to the existence of cross-cutting cleavages. Duverger agreed with Lipset, stressing that a two-party system is conducive to stable democracy because it is more moderate than a multiparty system. According to Duverger (1959: 388), 'the result [of multipartism] is an aggravation of political divisions and an intensification of differences ... a general "extremization" of opinion'. Such an exacerbation of partisan rivalry is not a characteristic of two-party systems.

The writings of Almond, Lipset and Duverger are characteristic of the literature of the pioneers of party systems theory in the 1950s and 1960s, which emphatically favoured the two-party system and argued that there is a negative relationship between the number of political parties and democratic stability. That is, the traditional literature on party systems claimed that democracy in heterogeneous societies with many parties simply did not work as well as it did in homogeneous societies with fewer parties. These scholars, among others such as Neumann (1956) and Dahl (1971), perceived that the two-party system was a necessary condition for political stability.[2] The existence of a third party between those on the left and the right, i.e. a centre party, would have been recognized as a crossing of the threshold of multipartism, hence bringing about a reduction of democratic stability.

However, a test of the two-party versus multiparty classification concerning the validity of the theory of democratic stability it proposes to represent results in failure. If the two-party category is supposed to include the stable democratic systems, and the multiparty category the unstable ones, then where does a stable multiparty system belong? More recent studies (Dodd, 1976; Laver, 1974; Lijphart, 1984; Midlarsky, 1984) have contradicted the traditional literature and demonstrated not only that a two-party format is not necessarily a condition for political stability, but that certain coalitions produced in multiparty systems can be as durable and stable as the one-party governments produced by two-party systems. These studies have, therefore, proven greater stability for multiparty systems than the traditional classification expected. For example, minimum winning coalitions in multiparty systems have been shown to be as durable and stable as the one-party governments produced in two-party systems. Thus, if stable multiparty systems exist, then a third party located in the centre could serve as a moderating force between the two opposing poles, rather than as a destabilizing factor.

There have been numerous attempts to develop more complex party system typologies. Two studies which have successfully refuted and corrected the idea that heterogeneity is conducive to instability are those of Lijphart (1977) and Sartori (1976). Both disagreed with previous scholars who stated that multipartism and instability are directly linked, and both adopted the same strategy to prove it: disaggregating the multiparty category. Furthermore, both pointed out that the destabilizing characteristic of multipartism is centrifugal electoral competition and its byproduct: polarization.

Lijphart modified the concern over homogeneous versus pluralistic political cultures by adding the effect of elite behaviour. The key to his entire classification scheme is that the effects of heterogeneity can be overcome by the mechanism of elite co-operation, thereby safeguarding stability in a multiparty environment otherwise conducive to instability: 'Consociational democracy means government by elite cartel designed to turn a democracy with a fragmented political culture into a stable democracy' (Lijphart, 1974: 79). Homogeneity, therefore, is not a necessary condition for stability; and fragmented political cultures – when they are consociational – can also be associated with democratic stability.

Sartori, too, made democratic stability his ultimate concern, but focused on the structure of party systems and their competitive dynamics. He divided the multiparty category into two different types, one stable – moderate pluralism – and the other unstable – polarized pluralism. The major difference between the stable pattern of moderate pluralism and the unstable features of polarized pluralism is the direction of competition. Centripetal systems, where competition is towards the political centre, are moderate and therefore stable.

Centrifugal systems, where competition is away from the centre and towards the extremes, are immoderate and unstable.

In summary, the traditional spectrum of party pluralism, perceived by the pioneers of party systems theory as a dichotomy between two-party and multiparty systems, has been criticized and replaced by the more recent literature. The essential distinction is no longer between two-party and multiparty systems, but rather between stable and unstable pluralism, which cuts across the traditionally undifferentiated multi-party category. The stable type of pluralism is associated with bipolar systems and characterized by centripetal (moderating) electoral competition, the unstable type with multipolar systems and centrifugal (polarizing) competition. The direction of competition is thus a result of the number of poles around which the party system pivots. Stable multiparty systems are bipolar. Unstable multiparty systems are multipolar, i.e. at least tripolar. The crucial difference between stable bipolarity and unstable multipolarity is that in the case of the former the system has no centre, only a left and a right pole, whereas this is not so for the latter, which possesses left, centre and right poles. Bipolar systems, therefore, display a moderate tendency of convergence towards the vacant centre, while multipolar systems reflect an extremist tendency of dispersal away from the occupied centre.

This study investigates and analyses the possibility that centripetal electoral drives and the existence of a centre are mutually exclusive – that the existence of a centre could serve as a cause for centrifugal competition. The goal is to assess if stable democracy, moderate electoral competition and bipolarity, on the one hand, and the existence of centre parties, on the other hand, are mutually exclusive. This study will, therefore, ask if we can truly conclude that only a multiparty system which lacks a strong centre can be an example of stable democracy.

1.3   Party Systems Typology and the Centre

The debate on the dynamic impact of the centre on party systems has two protagonists and remains to be settled. Duverger advocates the centre's moderating influence, while Sartori emphasizes its polarizing effect. According to Duverger, regardless of whether a centre party exists, there is no centre tendency – that is, no centripetal drives. It is appropriate to quote him in full:

> A duality of parties does not always exist, but almost always there is a duality of tendencies . . . This is equivalent to saying that *the centre does not exist in politics: there may well be a Centre party but there is no centre tendency, no*

centre doctrine. The term 'centre' is applied to the geometrical spot at which the moderates of opposed tendencies meet: moderates of the Right and moderates of the Left. Every Centre is divided against itself and remains separated by two halves, Left-Centre and Right-Centre. For the Centre is nothing more than the artificial grouping of the right wing of the Left and the left wing of the Right.... The dream of the Centre is to achieve a synthesis of contradictory aspirations; but synthesis is a power only of the mind. Action involves choice and politics involve action. (Duverger, 1959: 215, italics added)

This reasoning led Duverger to propose and accept the idea of natural political dualisms, and to conclude that two-party systems therefore 'correspond to the nature of things' (1959: 215). Furthermore, multi-partism is simply the result of an internal division of opinion and the subsequent splitting of the natural two-party system into extremists and moderates of both the right and the left. Multipartism, according to Duverger (1959: 229–30), thus does not possess a centre doctrine independent from the doctrines of the right or the left.[3]

Sartori disagreed with Duverger completely, arguing that there is such a thing as a centre tendency, but that it cannot exist simultaneously with a strong centre party. According to Sartori (1966: 159–60), the first distinctive feature of the unstable, polarized type of multi-partism is the physical existence of a centre. This means that the centre of the party system is occupied by one or a group of parties. The centre must now compete against both a left and a right pole, making the competitive mechanics of the system multipolar. This physical occupation of the centre is crucial because it implies that the moderate electorate, located at the centre of the political system, is no longer the floating electorate. It has become identified with a specific pole and is now a stable centre-voting electorate, taking the centre out of competition and pointing the direction of electoral competition away from the centre. Sartori summarized his argument as follows:

the very existence of a center party (or parties) discourages 'centrality,' i.e., the centripetal drives of the political system. And the centripetal drives are precisely the moderating drives. This is why this type is center-fleeting, or centrifugal, and thereby conducive to immoderate and extremist politics. (Sartori, 1976: 135)

Therefore, only when the moderate electorate located at the political centre is unidentified – because the centre is vacant, with the system lacking a centre party – can the party system be characterized by a centre tendency. That is to say, when there is no centre party, the parties' search for votes will move them towards the political centre –

centripetal competition. However, when a strong centre party exists, it is likely to offset such a convergence towards the centre. Sartori (1966: 156) argued that Duverger's statements should be reversed: 'A center opinion, or a center tendency, always exists in politics; what may not exist is a center party.' In short, centre tendencies are always present. They are facilitated and encouraged when there is no centre party, and obstructed when such a party exists.

The existence of a centre is, therefore, a contributing factor, even a causal factor, for either moderation or polarization – according to Duverger or Sartori, respectively. The case for moderation is intuitive, while the case for polarization is counter-intuitive. In order to settle the debate over the centre, one must assess whether an occupied centre can coexist with a centre tendency, or whether once the centre is no longer vacant polarization will begin. In other words, are the centre and polarization related?

1.4   Polarization and Government Stability

Polarization manifests a certain logic which pervades both the electorate and the political parties. The moderate electorate, in a polarized party system, perceives that the continued survival of the democratic system can be achieved only by excluding the extremist parties, specifically the anti-system ones, from power. The parties, meanwhile, limit access to government to the pro-system parties – that is, either those parties on the moderate centre-left, in the centre itself, or those on the moderate centre-right – leaving the parties on both the extreme left and extreme right out of contention. The result is a distinction between the governing-oriented pro-system parties and the alienated extremist parties, creating a limited 'semi-turnover' of governing parties (Daalder, 1971; Sartori, 1976; Ieraci, 1992).

Polarization has also been shown not only to determine the range of possible coalition partners, but also to hinder the actual formation of a cabinet, thereby impacting negatively on government durability. Lane and Ersson (1987), in their assessment of extra-parliamentary factors, pointed out that polarization is highly conducive to the fierce politicization of social problems, which is the most negatively correlated indicator of government durability. Dodd (1976) used factors endogenous to the parliamentary arena when he stated that the type of coalition formed is determined by the nature of the bargaining conditions that prevail within the party system. Information certainty concerning potential coalition partners and a willingness to bargain in order to enter a coalition are the two necessary conditions for the formation of a minimum winning coalition. Dodd found that this kind of coalition is the most durable in multiparty systems, and is as durable as one-party cabinets in two-party systems.[4] Fragmentation alone cannot hamper both vital conditions, but fragmentation and polarization together lessen both conditions, leading towards the formation of unstable, oversized coalitions. Midlarsky (1984) agreed with Dodd's conclusion, but saw a different cause, declaring that it is the centre-fleeing property of polarized multiparty systems which prevents the attainment of durable cabinets along the lines of a two-party system.

In short, moderate multipartism, despite its fragmentation, can impede the impact of polarization and maintain government stability. Polarized multipartism, buffeted by both fragmentation and polarization, hinders the possible formation of durable multiparty governments and is therefore unstable. Thus, when multiparty systems can avoid polarization, they prove able to build stable governments.

In attempting to pin-point which characteristic of polarization serves as the best indicator of democratic instability, scholars have concluded that multiparty systems are positively associated with instability only when extremist parties are present (Sanders and Herman, 1977; Powell, 1986). Support for extremist parties, therefore, appears to be the best barometer not only for the presence of polarization, but also for overall governmental stability.

Powell (1981) substantiates this point by elaborating a party system classification which distinguishes between empirically weak and strong party systems. The former have a sizeable contingent of extremist parties, with an average vote of over 15 per cent, whereas the latter lack any significant extremist parties. Powell's research concludes that stable governments are created by strong party systems – be they two-party or multiparty. Weak party systems, on the other hand, where support for extremist parties is substantial, are unable to produce stable governments.[5]

Support for extremist parties – indicated most clearly by the number of seats they hold – is thus the best predictor of government fragility (Taylor and Herman, 1971). The presence of extremist parties makes government difficult because it restricts the ideological spread of the party system from which a governmental majority can be formed. As their share of the seats increases, the share of the moderate parties decreases, making it likely that more parties need to be included in the coalition and thus impeding the task of building a stable government. That is, multipartism itself does not produce instability, but polarized multiparty systems – characterized by substantial support for extremist parties – are conducive to governmental instability.

1.5   The Centre and Government Stability

In a multiparty system, how does the existence of centre parties affect systemic polarization? Are strong centre parties conducive to government stability? Empirical research, as presented, has substantiated the fact that government stability is negatively associated with strong extremist parties. Moreover, sizeable extremist parties are positively associated with party system polarization. In short, government stability is negatively associated with polarization. One additional link could close the circle and present a comprehensive argument which includes the centre. This assertion, however, is based on a framework which has yet to be tested empirically, and is therefore only a theoretical claim: polarization is positively associated with the existence of a large centre party, or parties. Until this contention concerning the centre – proposed by Sartori – is validated, it would be presumptuous to conclude that the growth of the centre will impact negatively on government stability.[6] Moreover, this conclusion appears to run contrary to the intuitive conceptualization of the centre as a force of moderation.

According to Sartori's theory, there is a positive relationship between the centre and polarization:

> To be sure, the [party] system is center based precisely because it is polarized . . . . Nonetheless, it should not escape our attention that we are confronted here with a vicious whirl. In the long run a center positioning is not only a consequence but also a *cause* of polarization . . . . (Sartori, 1976: 135–6, italics in original)

Therefore, the existence of a centre is, in Sartori's framework, a contributing and causal factor for polarization.[7]

This does not mean that centre parties are not moderating or restraining factors. It does point out, though, that the counter-intuitive – or the alternative and equally intuitive – perception of the centre must be assessed. While this alternative perception does point out that not all centre parties foster heightened polarization – some actually do promote and sustain moderation – one function will prevail over the other. Which function will emerge as the dominant one is determined, at least in part, by the size of the centre parties. As long as the centre is a minor party, or group of parties, it functions in a moderating capacity within a stable bipolar party system. As the centre grows electorally, and is perceived to be strong by the other parties, it then furthers polarization and contributes to the rise of an unstable multipolar party system. The theoretical relationship between the centre and polarization must, therefore, be assessed empirically according to the size of the centre, and not just the presence of a centre. In other words, is a growth in the electoral strength of the centre associated with an increase in the level of party system polarization? If no such relationship is uncovered empirically, then the instability of governments due to extremist parties and polarization cannot be linked to the centre, whose intuitive moderating role will then be validated.

In summary, multipartism, both moderate and polarized, covers the overwhelming majority of contemporary democratic nations. The multiparty polities in which democracy has worked well are those characterized by low or moderate polarization, in spite of the fragmentation of the party system. Multipartism itself simply raises the need for government coalitions. There is nothing inherently unstable or dysfunctional in coalition government. Multiparty systems will therefore handicap democracy only if they are polarized. Working democracy and polarization are thus inversely related (Sani and Sartori, 1983).

If, and when, the centre encourages polarization, it is important to be able to explain why polarization is exacerbated. We thus need a model which accounts for the competitive trends leading to polarization, and in turn towards unstable governments. We can begin by asking if a centre-based party system exacerbates polarization, or quells it. Are only multiparty systems which lack a strong centre capable of government stability? Or, conversely, in order to be stable, does a multiparty system need the existence of a strong centre? The goal of this study is to settle the debate over whether the growth of centre parties abates or encourages polarization and its negative ramifications.

1.6 The Research Hypothesis and Agenda

A significant amount of the research on political parties has focused on measurable phenomena such as voting behaviour and electoral support. This has enabled political science scholars to use rigorously quantified and sophisticated data-processing techniques. These methods have helped overcome problems of interpretation and equivalence (Przeworski and Teune, 1970). Yet, as Mayer (1989) has pointed out, vote counting alone will not advance an explanation unless the data are integrated into and interpreted by a body of theory. If empirical research on electoral behaviour is to be significant, we must not only discern and delineate patterns and trends, but also present their causes and impacts in the form of testable hypotheses. Furthermore, arguments based on quantitative electoral evidence should be augmented with additional data, which are neither as rigorous nor as accessible. Ideology, for example, as reflected in the parties' programmes, can have an impact on the pattern of interaction among parties, and could thereby presumably be the cause of the electoral trends uncovered through the use of quantitative techniques.

The proposed research is thus based on assessing two contradictory theoretical frameworks which imply opposite correlations between systemic polarization and the strength of centre parties: the intuitive approach, which stresses the centre's moderating impact and hence a negative correlation with party system polarization, and the counter-intuitive, or alternative, approach, which points to the centre's positive correlation with systemic polarization. The aim is to systematically analyse the relationship between the strength of centre parties and the level of party system polarization, leading to a formulation of arguments which will validate one of the theoretical frameworks and enhance party systems theory.

The research hypothesis tests the empirical validity of the two opposing theories of centre parties and systemic polarization. The hypothesis, stated in the form of an empirical fact with theoretical underpinnings, is: *there is a relationship between the strength of the centre parties and the level of party system polarization.* A negative relationship would support the argument that the centre is a moderating factor conducive to stability, while a positive relationship will endorse the entire construct concerning the negative bearing of the centre on government stability.

This research focuses on the centre as the main variable *vis-à-vis* its relationship to systemic polarization and its impact on party competition. The hypothesis that this study seeks to validate is, therefore, based on the assumption that there is a causal relationship between the strength of centre parties and systemic polarization, and that this relationship will, in turn, impact on party competition. Given this implied logic, the hypothesis seeks to expose a certain sequence of events that are supposed to take place, i.e. a causal chain, as the growth of centre parties affects the party systems. In doing so, it not only uncovers the existence of a relationship between centre parties and party system polarization, but also assesses the cause of the relationship. That is, what drives the relationship in one or the other direction? Moreover, this study analyses the ramifications of the relationship for the state of electoral competition and its impact on government stability.

This study uses two complementary strategies, both an intensive and an extensive testing, to empirically analyse the previously elaborated causal theory. In the extensive analysis, data are collected and analysed from a variety of cases in the theory's presumed domain, and the hypothesis is tested in the attempt to assess the overall validity of the two opposing theories. In the intensive analysis, in which the hypothesis is retested and analysed in depth across two cases (chosen based on the findings produced by the extensive analysis), the explanatory power and predictive potential of the more conclusive theoretical framework is ascertained, and as a result party system theory relating to the centre is refined. This two-phased testing and analysis is aimed at achieving a two-tiered empirical validation, at first building confidence in a theoretical relationship, if it fits the extensive empirical data, and subsequently assuring its utility according to a more detailed fit to intensive case studies. The research strategy is thus designed to submit the theoretical frameworks to both statistical and systematic case analyses.

The empirical data examined in the extensive phase are national election results from European parliamentary democracies. The time-frame for this analysis is 1979 to 1989. Assuming that parties represent themselves quite similarly to the electorate across a timespan of one decade, the ideological positions of parties should be relatively stable during such a short period.[8] The second, intensive, phase is aimed at transforming the cross-national findings into functional theoretical assumptions, in order to refine party systems theory. The time-frame of the intensive case studies covers all post-war elections until 1990.

1.7 The Party Continuum, Positioning and Polarization

The dimension used to assess the degree of party system polarization, and the centre positioning of one or more parties, is the left–right ideological continuum. This research presupposes that polarization can be measured, and that political parties can be characterized in terms of their ideology and positions on a left–right scale.[9] That is to say that party system profiles can be generated and, subsequently, translated into quantitative scores. Moreover, this study's operationalization of both polarization and centre parties is based on a spatial notion of party systems and party competition.

Scholars have come to widely endorse spatial models as viable methods for political party analysis, but unidimensional spatial models, despite the supporting evidence, are not as broadly accepted. The case

for a unidimensional left–right continuum as advanced by Downs
(1957) – which this study endorses – is supported by a significant body
of evidence which shows that there is a single dominant left–right
dimension. Moreover, the left–right unidimensional ordering of parties is not simply a pure economic scale, but rather an overall dimension. Laponce (1981: 201) stated that 'Left/right is a general dimension linking together the religious, the economic, the political, and the
social.' Sani and Sartori concurred, stating that

> the left–right yardstick mirrors fairly well the voters' stands on some of
> the major conflict domains and echoes much of the voters' feelings
> towards significant political objects. And since its adoption not only
> simplifies the analysis but also enhances comparability, it seems to us that
> the advantages of relying on this measure largely outweigh its imperfec-
> tions. (Sani and Sartori, 1983: 314–16)

To this de Swaan added that

> the notion of a left–right scale to convey party space has been criticized as
> inadequate on several grounds ... but it appears to be sufficiently
> anchored in both the structure of the party system and the cognitive
> structure of ideology to be considered an independent variable in the
> context of social historical explanations. From the present evidence, it
> emerges as a powerful explanatory tool that, with its many hazards,
> deserves a more central role in empirical political theory. (de Swaan,
> 1973: 288–9)

Therefore, for the purpose of this research, the left–right unidimensional scale is adopted as a methodological tool, not only because of its
analytical validity, but also due to its analytical potential. It represents
not a duality, but a continuum, which has an obvious third element: a
centre, which is embedded within the polarity and can be used to
contrast the extremes to a middle ground.

There remains a pertinent open question: how does one place a
party's location on such a left–right scale? Several methods have been
used by scholars to achieve this goal. For example, parties have been
ordered according to: the self-location of their voters (Dalton, 1988);
the mean location of the party's members (Laponce, 1970); voting by
the parties while in parliament (Damgaard and Rusk, 1976); fundamental versus operative standards of the parties' ideology (Seliger,
1976); content analysis of party platforms (Thomas, 1982); ranking by
experts (Castles and Mair, 1984); and various other methods.

This research must assume that the distances between rank-points are
equivalent, while those between the parties are not. That is, the scale is

an interval level measurement, not a nominal or an ordinal one. An ordinal level scale would place the parties at equal intervals, assuming similar distances between all parties ranked along the scale. An interval scale, on the other hand, would be able to express relative distances between parties, thereby differentiating between a situation where, for example, the communist and socialist parties are rather close, and one where they are distant. In other words, an interval level scale can account for the ideological distance that separates parties, be it large or small. Such a scale would have two additional properties. First, the relative distance of the parties from the extremes would be comparable. That is, the most extreme left and extreme right parties would not define the ends of the scale, but would be placed at distances from the ends relative to other such extreme parties in other party systems. The unidimensional left–right scale that this study adopts is thus a party-inferred space, not a party-defined space – the parties are not at the ends but are points within the space. As the intensity of the ideological space of competition varies, this change can be described in spatial terminology.

The second additional property is that the relative distance between the parties, which has major ramifications for party competition, should show which parties are close to each other and which are not. Those parties with minor distances between them can allow for vote transfers, coalition formation, and therefore inter-party competition. On the other hand, those with a large distance, or a disjointed space, between them do not allow for any vote transfers or coalition formations, and also do not compete with each other. Extremist parties possess such a disjointed space between themselves and the pro-system parties, which partially explains why they compete centrifugally and not centripetally.

This study adopts the location of parties along the left–right scale elaborated by Castles and Mair (1984), who ascertain the location of parties based on views of country experts. Respondents were asked to place all of the parties represented in their national parliaments on an ideological 10-point scale ranging from 0 representing the ultra-left, to 10 representing the ultra-right.[10] In assembling their 'expert' data, they encountered no tendency to spread the parties in such a way as to fill up the scale. This showed that each party system was being judged by general standards, rather than by purely national considerations. The time-frame at which this scale was produced, 1984, falls in the exact chronological mid-point of the extensive cross-national analysis, making the scale extremely appropriate. Such a measure of party ranking thus fulfils the requirements raised above. Furthermore, the comparative potential of such a scale enhances the ability to create a cross-national measure of polarization – which links back to party system theory, since distribution and polarization along the left–right scale has been associated with government instability and breakdown (Dahl, 1966: 371–86).

Polarization and centre parties are thus the two main variables in this study, and the notion of both is based on a unidimensional spatial analysis of party systems. In the case of polarization, different measures have been elaborated over time. Mass survey data and techniques have improved these measures, afforded easier access and facilitated their use for comparative research. However, there still appears to be a lexical confusion and disorder concerning the concept of polarization in the literature.

For the purpose of this research, a measure of polarization is developed which focuses on the parliamentary strength of parties, not their electoral strength. The measure will, therefore, be based on the percentage of the seats won by each party in the lower house of parliament, and will thus not include parties without parliamentary representation. The respective ideological positions of each party on the left–right scale will be taken from the previously elaborated continuum based on expert judgements. Parties with parliamentary seats which do not appear on this continuum will be ranked by the author, based on current literature. Studies have already appeared using this scale to measure polarization (Crepaz, 1990; van Roozendaal, 1990),[11] and party systems scholars have argued that just such left–right locations are the best way to measure polarization (Sani and Sartori, 1983: 310–16).

Each party's percentage of parliamentary seats will be multiplied by its position on the left–right scale and summed to produce a weighted party system mean of left–right seat distributions for a particular national election. The left–right positions of each party will then have the weighted system mean of seat distributions, for that election, deducted from it. The results for all of the parties will be summed to produce a measure of party system polarization for a particular country after an election. Therefore, the left–right polarization of a party system will be assessed in this study according to the following formula:

$$\text{Polarization} = \sum_{i=1}^{N} p_i (x_i - \overline{x})^2$$

where N is the number of parties in the system, p_i is the percentage of the seats won by each party, x_i is the respective left–right ideological position of each party, and $\bar{x}$ is the weighted system mean of the left–right seat distribution for that election.

The result of this measure of polarization, for each national election, will be correlated with the parliamentary size of the centre parties. Chapter 2 discusses and defines the meaning of centre parties.

Notes

1. See also Almond and Powell (1966).
2. For a discussion of the case for two-party systems, and a critique of two-party theory, see Lijphart (1984), Chapter 7.
3. There is another possibility for multipartism to arise, according to Duverger: the overlapping of cleavages. However, this is still based on mutual sets of independent antitheses (Duverger, 1959: 231–4).
4. Lijphart (1984: 275) substantiates this and argues further that the differences in cabinet durability between types of multiparty coalitions, specifically minimal winning and oversized coalitions, are greater than the difference between the one-party cabinets of a two-party system and coalition cabinets.
5. See also Powell (1982).
6. The only empirical study of the relationship between polarized pluralism and the associated characteristics Sartori identifies finds that there is no evidence of centrifugal trends in polarized party systems (Powell, 1987). However, the study perceives stable levels of polarization, and therefore no change in the parliamentary strength of centre parties or anti-system parties. There is no discussion of a decrease or increase in the level of polarization, which, according to Sartori's theory, would then impact on the strength of both anti-system and centre parties.
7. In an earlier version of his typology, Sartori (1966: 156) elaborated on the consequence and cause of centre positioning: 'As a consequence that reflects the existence of a polarized society the center party is mainly a feed-back of the centrifugal drives which predominate in the system. As a causal factor it is precisely the existence of a center party which feeds the system with centrifugal strains.'
8. Powell (1986) agreed that party positions can be relatively stable over a 10-year period, and also used a fixed 10-year measure for statistical analysis in assessing the impact of extremist parties on cabinet instability.
9. Numerical ideological characterization scales of political parties are presented by various scholars and organizations. For example: the US State Department publishes data on party strengths using a code ranging from 1, communist, to 4, conservative; the Eurobarometer surveys use a 10-point scale to rank parties; Dodd's (1974) scale covers 14 points; and Janda (1975) presents a 40-point scale.
10. A similar method of ordering parties along an ideological dimension also used expert judgements, but collated the information from several specialist studies published on each country (Taylor and Laver, 1973).
11. Crepaz (1990) attempted to measure polarization as the distance between the two most extreme parties using the Castles and Mair continuum. Such a measure yields very crude results because it does not take into consideration the weights of the parties.

2

What is a Centre Party?

2.1 Conceptualizing the Centre

Dualities and polarities create a categorical contrast, embedded within logical structures, that has shaped the development of comparative analysis. Yet Hindu philosophy teaches that while the world of contradictions is at the peripheries, the essential truth that reconciles these differences is in the centre. Thinking in threes, as opposed to twos, is almost as frequent and natural, which has led scholars to negate the assumed universal applicability of polarities. Dual divisions represent an ideal which is constantly and continuously defeated by empirical evidence, leading to the conclusion that a third term, in a mediating role, must be added to the original dualities. Marx and Hegel considered thesis and antithesis, which led them to synthesis. Freud postulated a theory based on the id, the ego and the superego. Plato divided society into the three classes of commoners, guardians and philosophers. Modern politics distinguishes between executive, legislative and judiciary. Triads are, therefore, as natural – and seemingly more logical – than dyads. Dyads, especially the left-right universal dyad of politics, have an obvious and embedded third element within their polarity – the centre.

The centre has been criticized as being either a shallow opportunistic position, or a place to be crushed from both sides. As accurate as this criticism might be, it does not do justice to centre ideology, or to the implications of a centre positioning. In both France and England, after the Napoleonic wars, proponents of centre ideology attempted to establish middle-class rule as a golden mean between the extremes of revolution and reaction. Prominent philosophers and politicians have contemplated the centre and raised ideas concerning its background and essence. In France, the two most prominent centre theorists were the Doctrinaires Pierre Paul Royer-Collard and François Pierre Guillaume Guizot. In England, centre doctrine was advanced by the Reform Whigs, and elaborated by two of their members, Henry Peter Brougham and Thomas Babington Macaulay (Starzinger, 1965).

In more contemporary times, political parties in numerous parliamentary democracies have adopted the centre label. But are these centre parties in name indeed centre parties? And if so, what type of centre parties are they? Regretfully, at present there is a lexical confusion surrounding centre parties in the literature, and in practice, which is based on the indiscriminate use of the term 'centre', as well as the lack of an appropriate classification of this category.

Party systems scholars have a tendency to attach the centre label all too quickly and superficially, and have thereby emptied it of any apparent meaning. For example, a 'centre-based' party system is one that constantly relies on 'centre parties' in the process of coalition-making, producing either centre–left or centre–right coalitions. Actually, it depends on whether we are referring to ideologically positioned *centre* parties or spatially located *middle* parties in this context as to whether both types of coalitions are possible, which points to an inadequacy in the concept and definition of the term 'centre-based' party system. A party system with an ideologically positioned centre party can lack parties on one flank of the centre, thus making the process of coalition-making unidirectional. A party system with a spatially located middle party, on the other hand, will by definition have significant parties on both right and left, opening coalition possibilities on both flanks.

We must acknowledge that by simply assigning a party to the centre category – or, still worse, accepting the party label as a defining characteristic – we lump different types of centre parties into one ambiguous category without much clarity or purpose. Each type of centre party is different, functioning in a specific manner, and presenting distinct and sometimes contrary consequences for the party system.

In short, proponents of centre ideology, from Aristotle in ancient Greece to the Doctrinaires in post-Napoleonic France and the Reform Whigs in Britain, have attempted to establish middle-class rule as a golden mean between the extremes. However, in the accumulated contemporary academic literature there are few explicit references to the concept of a centre, and even fewer attempts to define and study the centre. Apart from Duverger (1959) and Sartori (1976), only Downs (1957) and Daalder (1984) have included the centre as an important variable in their theoretical discussion of party systems.

The Downsian model based party equilibrium largely on voter distribution, and the dynamics of party ideologies are perceived as the originating factors in the appearance of a centre party. The emergence of a centre is thus the result of two factors: first, the maintenance of a normal unimodal distribution in the electorate; and second, a growing distance between the parties on both right and left. In other words, ideological party polarization without an accompanying trend in the electorate can bring about the breakdown of a two-party system, and the rise of a third party in the newly created centre area (Downs, 1957: 127–32).

Daalder (1984), on the other hand, delved into the various definitions of the centre, theoretically and empirically, and presented a critique of the concept. He suggested that the literature offers few cumulative lessons concerning the centre, because the term has been employed ambiguously. The centre can mean either a location in a political space, a mechanic of holding the balance of power, or a middle position based on specific cleavages. That is, the centre can be a theoretical point to which parties may be close or far, or it can be an actual party. According to Daalder, there are no specific conditions accepted by political scientists in general that define a centre.[1]

This is as far as the scholarly literature in political science has gone in its discussion of the centre and centre parties. Other fields, such as sociology and geography, have focused on the centre, but their conceptualization is entirely different (i.e. centre versus periphery). However, quite recently, there have been a few political scientists who have begun to devote attention once again to the centre and to centre parties, such as van Roozendaal (1990), Ieraci (1992), Scully (1992) and Keman (1994). Nevertheless, the recent articles on centre parties continue the indiscriminate usage of the term, stretching its meaning to encompass from, on the one hand, all non-extremist parties to, on the other hand, an important actor which could be any party, extremist or not.[2] It would thus appear that Daalder's concluding statements are still correct today.

> We clearly need an explicit study of normative assessments of center parties. We have frequently drawn attention to the many unspecified value judgments associated with the treatment of notions like center and center parties. A careful review of such value judgments might help us to obtain clearer insights into alternative theories of good government,

which after all lay a heavy hand on our discussions and comparative research on the empirical functioning of party systems. (Daalder, 1984: 108)

Scully's more recent study of party politics in Chile, which focused on the impact of the centre, points out that the explicit study of centre parties which Daalder called for over a decade ago has yet to be undertaken.

> Since a principle theoretical issue ... concerns the controversial role of center parties within multiparty systems ... the role played by the political center is more complex than is commonly acknowledged and requires rethinking .... In light of earlier arguments regarding the role of the center ... the emergence and behavior of center parties require reappraisal. (Scully, 1992: 3–4)

This chapter seeks to rectify the present dearth of conceptual clarity surrounding centre parties. It aims to present an explicit conceptualization of centre parties, and to propose a new classification. It will illustrate examples of the main types of centre parties proposed by using data from the Italian, German, Swedish, Danish, Dutch and Belgian party systems.

2.2   Defining the Centre

There are two important distinctions that must be made when considering the use of the term centre party, in order to eliminate the existing ambiguity. These distinctions concern the concepts centre and middle on the one hand, and the terms median, pivot and central on the other.

First, is the party, or parties, in the centre or in the middle? A centre is identifiable by the end-points of the ideological scale, or continuum, being used. The middle, on the other hand, is identified by the existence of opposing poles – usually left and right. Therefore, the centre is the point located at equal distances from the (theoretical) ends of the scale, whereas the middle is located between the (empirical) competing poles of a specific party system.

When we use the term centre, we should not define the party system continuum in terms of parties particular to that specific system. The most extreme left and extreme right parties should not define the ends of the scale, but should be placed at distances from the ends relative to extreme parties in other party systems. The scale should be an ideologically defined cross-national continuum, where similar parties from different countries are located at congruent points within the scale.

Castles and Mair (1984) produced such a scale by assessing the location of parties based on the views of country experts. Respondents were asked to place parties on an ideological 10-point continuum. Centre parties were then defined as those parties located between 3.75 and 6.25 on the scale produced. Each party system was thus judged and described using general standards, rather than purely national considerations. A centre party is, therefore, ideologically positioned in the centre of a fixed, universal, ideological left–right continuum. This type of party, by being ideologically located using general criteria, can also be identified ideologically. That is, all centre parties should have certain shared ideological characteristics, such as being ideologically moderate by objective international standards. Moreover, beyond their ideological congruence, centre parties are distinguishable from non-centre parties based on programmatic differences, and hence comprise a universalistic *famille spirituelle* (Keman, 1994).

When using the term middle, we move from one level of analysis to another. Middle is a country-specific concept, and carries little or no equivalence value for cross-national purposes, other than descriptive or mechanical elements. The party system continuum need not be defined by general standards, and the most extreme parties can define the endpoints. What is important here is the identification of the major poles of electoral competition, and the location of the middle between these two. This does not mean that the middle is simply the area between the two largest parties, because these two parties may not represent the major poles of electoral competition. In most cases the two biggest parties do indeed represent the major poles – as exhibited by the Communists and Christian Democrats in the Italian case, until 1993 – but a smaller party may lie further to the right, or to the left, of one of the two biggest parties and still represent one of the two competing poles – illustrated by the Dutch Liberals. That is, the middle is the area between the opposing alternatives of the major cleavage in the politics of a particular country.[3] In addition, a pole can be composed of more than one party. If two parties are very closely allied, making it impossible to form a governing coalition with only one, then both must be considered as forming the same pole. For example, the Rally for the Republic and the Union for French Democracy in France would constitute one pole, whereas the Communist Party and the Socialist Party do not.

The middle can thus be different types of parties from one country to another – liberal, socialist, religious, agrarian, radical, social democrat, green, etc. – representing no equivalent cross-national ideological characteristics. If the two main poles of electoral competition are very distant from each other, then there will be a large middle area. Those parties closer to one of the poles than to the middle line will still constitute the middle, unless they become so closely attached to one of the poles that they become part of it. In other words, as long as the party is a viable coalition partner for either pole, and perceives itself as such, it is a middle party. Moreover, the middle can move from one party to another within a specific country over time as the ideological space of electoral competition changes. What Sartori wrote concerning centre parties is, therefore, more appropriate for middle parties:

> What matters is neither the name nor the doctrine (whatever a center doctrine may be) but the position ... since a center is relative to its left and right wings, it will follow in the long run the general trend of the polity. If history goes to the left, the center can only remain in a central position if it also moves left (and vice versa if history goes to the right) ... the center will move if the balance between its left and its right should shift. (Sartori, 1966: 157, 164–5)

In short, the definition of a middle party is ideologically blind. However, most middle parties do share attitudinal characteristics, such as fear of a grand coalition between right and left.

In the simplest terms, the centre is a fixed, party-inferred concept, whereas the middle is an intermediate, party-defined term. That is, a centre party can exist without a party on the left, the right, or both, whereas a middle party can exist only if parties to both its left and to its right exist. Moreover, the identification of a middle party requires and depends on the *a priori* definition of the major poles of electoral competition.

Once the difference between centre and middle parties is clear, a second distinction must be made between centre and middle parties on the one hand, and median, pivot or central parties on the other. A party can be all five, but the literature incorrectly assumes that median, pivot or central parties are automatically centre (and middle) parties as well.

A median party can be defined as either the party that possesses the median legislator in parliament, with no majority to its right or to its left, or the party that is surrounded by a similar number of parties on both its right and its left. Both definitions are based on a particular arrangement of the parties and their members.

According to the first definition – the party with the median legislator – the median party would not necessarily be a centre party; and the median party could not be a middle party if the party system were either two-party or multiparty with a majority party. The median legislator would in both cases belong to the majority party, which could be positioned in the ideological centre of the party system, but could not be the middle party between the two major poles of conflict. For example, the Conservative Party in Britain held a majority in the House of Commons from the late 1970s to the late 1990s, and thus possessed the median legislator. Despite its movement, after replacing Margaret Thatcher with John Major, towards the centre, few would consider it to be a centre party, and because it represents one of the major poles of competition it cannot be a middle party.

In the second definition – an equal number of parties surrounding the median party – the median party is also not necessarily either a centre or a middle party. For example, most Scandinavian party systems are characterized by a strong social democratic party on the left, and a plethora of bourgeois parties on the right. The median party in these cases could be located among the moderate right bourgeois bloc, thus being outside the centre; and, since this bloc represents one of the major poles, the median party will also be outside the middle. For the term median to be relevant in the discussion of both centre and middle parties, it must be restricted to multiparty systems in which no party possesses a majority, or to a party surrounded by a similar number and size of parties on both right and left.

The pivotal party, largely an equilibrium-related functional term, has not been defined uniformly. It can be identified as anything from an indispensable party for the formation or survival of a coalition, to a party that holds a number of seats higher than the difference between the seats held by the parties to the right and to the left (Rémy, 1975). The former definition need not exclude extremist parties whose defection from the coalition would bring about its collapse – not to mention moderate right and left parties with the same attribute – and is not related to centre or middle parties. The latter definition, which takes both size and location into account, is quite close to the definition of a middle party, but need not refer to a centre party if electoral competition is not spread out evenly across the continuum.

A central party has also not been strictly defined and need not coincide with the concept of either a centre or a middle party. A party is central according to its degree of relevance, i.e. its share of seats, based on the issue at stake. Hence, the characterization of a party as central can stretch from one extreme of constant indispensability to another of mere potential should a particular scenario develop. A central party can thus be any party in the party system, based on a conjectural constellation.

This study, therefore, suggests that the terms median and central be excluded from the classification of centre and middle parties, but that the term pivotal party be included. Furthermore, while the pivotal concept cannot define a centre or middle party, it can be used as an added criterion to already delineated centre and middle parties. That is, only when a party has already been identified as a centre or middle party can the term pivot be meaningfully added, in order to ascertain the party's function in the party system.[4]

The classification of centre, as opposed to middle, parties which this study proposes is the following.

1. *Centre party* : an ideologically positioned party which occupies the metrical centre of an ideological continuum, or is near it. A centre party will thus be located at a relatively equal geometric distance from each end of an ideologically defined cross-national scale, and will not need to be flanked by other parties. The centre is equivalent from one country to another – centre parties from different countries are located at congruent points along the scale – and possesses several shared cross-national characteristics.
   1a. *Pivotal centre party* : a centre party that has no parliamentary majority to either its right or its left.
2. *Middle party* : a spatially located party between the two opposing poles of the party system. A middle party will thus be located in between the major poles of electoral competition of a country-specific continuum, and defined only in terms of such poles existing on both right and left flanks of the middle. The middle carries no cross-national ideological equivalence – it can be a different type of party from one system to another and can switch from one party to another within one system over time – but only descriptive relevance and attitudinal predispositions.
   2a. *Pivotal middle party* : a middle party that has no parliamentary majority to either its right or its left.

Both types of parties can coexist in the same party system, separately or as one party. The pivotal function can belong to either, or to neither. Furthermore, the definitions above incorporate two caveats: first, they are unidimensional in their elaboration; and second, they assume that parties are unitary actors. These two caveats can be overcome by either specifying the use of a multidimensional analysis – which can produce a multidimensional centre or middle party, a centre party on one dimension which is a middle party on another, a middle party along one axis but not along another, etc. – or by dropping the unitary actor assumption and mapping centre and middle actors which are not necessarily parties, i.e. factions.

2.3   Centre Parties in European Party Systems

In order to elaborate and exhibit the distinction between centre and middle parties, this study presents an in-depth analysis of the Italian party system, from 1946 to 1993. Keeping in mind this distinction, an analysis of the German party system, from 1949 to 1987, will show the possible overlap of these two party types. Finally, a comparison of middle parties will elaborate the country-specific context of this type, as opposed to the cross-national character of centre parties.

Farneti wrote that when analysing the post-war Italian party system

> both bi-polar and three-polar models are legitimate. The difficulties and ambiguities for the analysis of Italian electoral history derive from the fact that both models ... form the ground of different and plausible explanations, because they both have empirical foundations. (Farneti, 1985: 86)

This quote succinctly illustrates the confusion surrounding the possible descriptions of the Italian party system.[5] The leading proponent of Italian bipolarity was Galli (1966, 1975). According to Galli's model, Italy could have been perceived as an 'imperfect two-party system' despite its multiple parties. Galli saw Italy's party system as simply being tilted to the left. That is, the Italian Communist Party (PCI), rather than a social democratic party, represented the working class while the Christian Democrats (DC), rather than a conservative party, represented the bourgeoisie. The principal advocate of Italian multipolarity was Sartori (1966, 1976). Sartori saw post-war Italy as the prototypical case of 'polarized pluralism'. Italy's multipolar party system featured a strong centre pole dominating the small pro-system parties located on both right and left, flanked by anti-system parties, from neo-fascists to communists, comprising the extreme poles. What was not in dispute between scholars was that the two major forces of Italian politics were Catholicism and communism. These two forces represented the political subcultures that progressively established powerful parties in Italian politics from the 1920s until the 1990s.

The important distinction between these two approaches, for the purpose of this study, is which parties represented which poles. That is, as Table 2.1 shows, a bipolar configuration places the PCI and the DC at

Table 2.1 Two approaches to party poles in Italy

	Bipolarity	Multipolarity
Left	PCI, PR, PSI	PCI, PR
Centre		PSI, PSDI, DC, PRI
Right	PSDI, PRI, DC, PLI, MSI-DN	PLI, MSI-DN

Parties appear from left to right according to their ranking on the ideological continuum

PCI, Italian Communist Party; PR, Radical Party; PSI, Italian Socialist Party; PSDI, Italian Social Democratic Party; PRI, Italian Republican Party; DC, Christian Democrats; PLI, Italian Liberal Party; MSI-DN, Monarchists and Neo-Fascists.

opposite ends of the party spectrum, with each clearly located as the major parties of the left and right pole respectively. A multipolar alignment, on the other hand, puts the DC and its small peripheral parties, the Italian Social Democratic Party (PSDI) and the Italian Republican Party (PRI), at the centre pole, with the Italian Liberal Party (PLI) together with the Monarchists and Neo-Fascists (MSI-DN) comprising a much smaller right pole. Nonetheless, in an analysis of the Italian party system, both the bipolar and multipolar configurations place the PCI and the DC as the major poles of party competition.

The main question that concerns us here is not the number of poles, but rather whether the DC is a centre party or a middle party. As Barnes (1977: 104) wrote, 'the right, though well represented in parties, is weak in numbers. But its existence is a prerequisite for the center position of the DC.' One must disagree on two counts. First, the existence of a right pole is a prerequisite for a middle location, not a centre position. Second, in order for a middle location to exist, the right cannot be weak, but must be a major pole. Therefore, to correct Barnes, the DC can be centrally positioned regardless of whether the right is strong, weak or absent. However, if the right is weak, or absent, then the centre position of the DC cannot simultaneously be a middle location.

According to the overwhelming majority of party mappings, the DC is considered a centre party. In that case, the centre in Italy is a major pole, whereas the right is not, and hence the middle must be found between this major pole and the other major pole – the PCI-dominated left pole. Tarrow (1977: 199) has pointed out that 'there was always a small but influential "third force" that was never successfully colonized by either Marxism or Catholicism and served as a buffer between Left and Right'. Indeed, the Italian Socialist Party (PSI) has traditionally been in the middle of Italian politics, as have the PSDI and PRI. The PSI's strategy – at least under Craxi – was directed at becoming not only a middle party but, having broken off from the left pole, by moving towards the centre, at becoming a centre party, if not a pivotal centre party (Pasquino, 1986).

However, the DC's influence over both moderate and conservative voters had made it *de facto* the conservative party. The DC had indeed taken steps to court the right at times – for example, in 1960, the DC went so far as to form a government enjoying only neo-fascist support, and after the 'Hot Autumn' of 1969, it moved to the right again during the 'strategy of tension' phase – but then usually retreated back towards the centre, as in its subsequent acceptance of the 'historical compromise'. A chronological perspective would thus lead to several alternating descriptions of the Italian party system, which serve to elucidate the difference between and identification of centre and middle parties. For example, the DC could be perceived as a party that crossed back and forth across the threshold of the centre ideological area, at times belonging to the moderate right, but always comprising the major party of the centre-right pole. The PSI spent its first post-war decade being a close ally of the PCI in an extreme left position, but over the next decade slowly detached itself and became a middle party, resting between the two major poles of party competition, finally shifting into the centre itself. Table 2.2 presents several phases of these, and other, party movements in post-war Italy. It is designed to illustrate how the movement of parties along the left–right continuum affected their placement in either the centre or middle category, or both, but not to offer a comprehensive or precise description.

The phases in Table 2.2 are combined and presented in Figure 2.1, thereby illustrating the difference between centre and middle parties, the specific parties that fall into each category at any particular period, and the overlap of the two categories.[6]

Table 2.2 Centre and middle parties in the Italian party system

Phase	Description	Centre parties	Middle parties
1	DC–PCI bipolarity	DC, PRI	PRI
2	PSDI splits from PSI	DC, PSDI, PRI	PSDI, PRI
3	PSI detaches from PCI	DC, PSDI, PRI	PSI, PSDI, PRI
4	DC moves right	PSDI, PRI	PSI, PSDI, PRI
5	DC returns to centre	DC, PSDI, PRI	PSI, PSDI, PRI
6	PSDI moves right of DC	DC, PSDI, PRI	PSI, PRI
7	PSDI moves left of DC	DC, PSDI, PRI	PSI, PSDI, PRI
8	PR leap-frogs over PCI	DC, PSDI, PRI	PSI, PSDI, PRI, PR
9	PSI moves to centre	DC, PSI, PSDI, PRI	PSI, PSDI, PRI, PR
10	PLI moves to centre	DC, PSI, PSDI, PRI, PLI	PSI, PSDI, PRI, PR

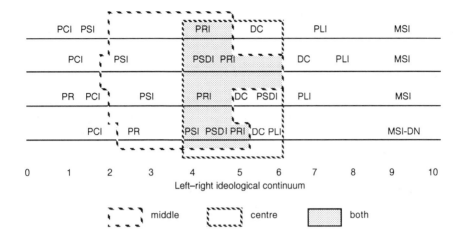

Figure 2.1 Centre and middle parties in the Italian party system, 1946–93
Note: The progression of the time-line is from top to bottom

Centre parties are defined as all parties that fall between 4 and 6 on an ideological cross-national 10-point left–right scale, based on the locations assigned to these parties by country experts. Middle parties are all of the parties located between the two poles of the party system, exemplified by the PCI and DC (the only exception is the PSI during the first period, which, due to a 'unity pact' with the PCI, could not be perceived as separate and therefore remained outside the sphere of middle parties). Figure 2.1 exhibits two of the five possible combinations (i) and (iii) of middle and centre parties. The middle can consist of those parties which are: (i) the entire group of centre parties along with additional non-centre parties; (ii) the entire group of centre parties; (iii) some of the centre parties along with other non-centre parties; (iv) a sub-group of the centre parties; or (v) none of the centre parties.

Parties can cross into or out of the centre (ideological) area by a simple movement along the left–right continuum. However, for a party to move into the middle (spatial) area of the continuum it must either: (1) detach itself from one of the poles and move towards the other; (2) leap-frog from outside one of the poles into the middle area; or (3) come into being between the two poles. The first instance was demonstrated by the PSI, the second by the Radical Party (PR), and the third by the PSDI.

The concepts of median and pivot are quite clear in Italy. The DC won approximately 40 per cent of the seats in the post-war elections, until 1994, while neither the parties to its left nor the ones to its right ever achieved a majority. The DC was, therefore, the party with the median legislator, as well as the pivotal party. The concept of a central party is not as clear. Due to the extreme multiparty nature of the Italian party system, practically every party, at one time or another, was relevant to an important issue at stake, and could have been perceived as central. A centre label party is the only type of centre party that has not appeared in the Italian party system thus far.

Figure 2.2 represents the positions of the three main German parties, the Social Democratic Party (SPD), the Christian Democratic Union

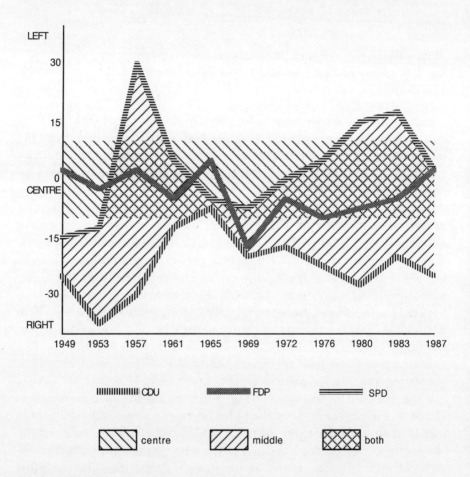

Figure 2.2 Centre and middle parties in the German party system, 1949–87. Data from Laver and Budge (1992)

(CDU) and the Free Democratic Party (FDP).[7] For the sake of illustration, the centre has been designated as the area between +10 and −10. The two main poles of electoral competition in Germany were the SPD and CDU, and thus the middle was the area between them. The figure shows the difference between centre and middle, which affects all three main parties, and the overlap of these two party concepts.

Figure 2.2 shows that in the first two post-war elections, and in 1965, there was no middle party in Germany, although there was a centre party. Only after 1953 did the area between the two major poles expand to encompass the FDP, and it thus became the middle party as well. In 1965 the middle contracted, and the FDP remained only a centre party, along with the SPD and CDU. By the following election it regained the middle location, but moved out of the centre position, only to regain it both in 1972 and henceforth. That is, the FDP had always been a centre party, apart from 1969, but not always a middle party. The FDP shows, at different periods, that a party can be only a centre party, both a centre and middle party, or only a middle party. In the mid-1960s, all three major German parties were centre parties, but there was no middle party. In short, during a majority of the post-war period Germany had two centre parties, but never less than one; whereas it has had one middle party for most of this period, but at times none.

Figure 2.3 presents a cross-national perspective of middle parties: the Swedish Centre Party (CP), the Danish Radical Liberals (RV), the Dutch Catholic Party (KVP/CDA), the Belgian Christian Socialist Party (PSC) and the Italian Socialist Party (PSI). All of the parties mapped in this figure are located between the major poles of party competition in their respective countries. The point here is to illustrate how divergent the ideologies of middle parties can be, and that they do not correspond to the ideological boundaries which delineate centre parties.

As Figure 2.3 shows, not one of the middle parties from five different countries was also a centre party during the entire post-war period. On the contrary, middle parties stray out of the ideological centre as much as they remain inside it. The separation between these two classes of parties reached its climax in the early 1970s, when none of the five middle parties was a centre party. Moreover, apart from a general shift to the right, followed by a return to the centre, there is no unified ideological tendency that is shared by middle parties at any period. While some middle parties move to the right, others move to the left, and vice versa. The distance between middle parties is similar to, and at times larger than, that between the two major poles of competition in any one country. In short, apart from a very general trend, with severe

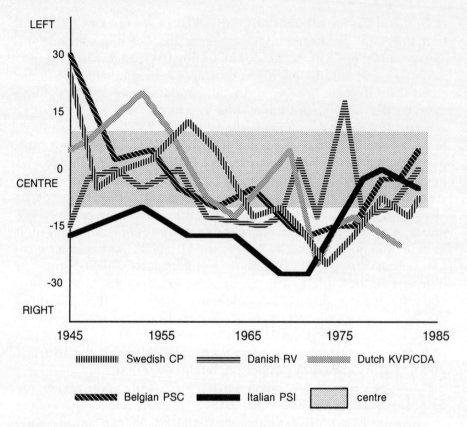

Figure 2.3 Middle parties in comparative perspective. Data from Laver and Budge (1992)

fluctuations, there is no ideological pattern that middle parties exhibit cross-nationally.

Italy provides a case in point; during the 1980s the centre came to incorporate five parties – every one of the pro-system parties, but not all of them middle parties – turning it into a very crowded area (Figure 2.1). The Italian experience thus clearly shows not only that it is necessary to define the centre in clearer terminology, but that another concept needs to be added in order to afford a better description of the party system. Armed with improved conceptual tools, we can present a more precise description concerning what was, and still is, an in-herently complicated and changing party system. Moreover, the new conceptualization of centre parties, and the delineation of middle parties, will benefit the comparative analysis of party systems in general.

2.4 Theoretical Consequences

There are two main, and one minor, types of centre party which the literature has failed to distinguish. The minor type is simply a centre label party, a party that carries the word 'centre' in its name. This group includes such parties as the ideologically centrist Centre Party that exists in Finland, Norway and Sweden, and the Centre Democrats in Denmark, but it also encompasses such moderate right parties as the now defunct Union of the Democratic Centre in Spain, and even extreme right parties such as the Centre Party in The Netherlands. The first main type is an *ideologically positioned centre party*, a party that occupies or is near the metrical centre of an ideological continuum. If a party system is ideologically described using a 10-point left–right scale, the centre parties would be those at or near 5 (say between 4 and 6). The second main type of centre party is the *spatially located middle party*, a party between the two opposing poles of the party system. A spatially defined middle party can serve as a voter-exchange party, a resting place for voters discontented with one of the two major adversaries but unable to swing to the other pole.

The attempt to reclassify and delineate between centre and middle parties leads to some preliminary conclusions. First, specific parliamentary constellations over time in one country can be as relevant for an analysis of the centre, and the middle, as in several different countries. Second, coalition theorists should find much promise in the middle party concept, especially those who incorporate the ideology variable when analysing the coalition's range. Third, the classification of party systems focusing on the presence, number, size and behaviour of centre and middle parties, as opposed to the other characteristics, could provide an entirely new perspective. Fourth, the floating vote, traditionally identified in the literature as being in the centre, need not be in the centre at all and is associated much more with middle parties than with centre parties. Fifth, the link between systemic polarity, electoral patterning, party goals and the encouragement of a particular kind of centre can shed much light on the treatment of the centre concept, and provide clearer insights into alternative theories of these variables. For example, the following two general models can be suggested:

1. Multipolarity → ideological patterning → policy-seeking parties → centre position.
2. Bipolarity → pragmatic patterning → office-seeking parties → middle location.

That is, a middle location could be the result of a party attempting to station itself between the major poles of electoral competition in an attempt to gain office, and thereby being more flexible concerning its policy positions, because it must function in a bipolar (not necessarily a two-party) system. A centre position, on the other hand, could be the result of more rigid partisanship – and thereby reduced flexibility in the quest for coalition potential – in order to avoid risking the loyalty of the party's ideologically committed followers, while being surrounded by numerous other equally intractable opponents. These conclusions are only a preliminary assessment of how the proposed conceptual delineation of the centre and the middle can improve the comparative study of party systems.

Daalder correctly stated that the idea of a centre has been perceived as an attractive one by politicians, who in recent decades have regarded the very word centre as a positive label for their parties.

> Yet, there is practically no systematic treatment of the center or of center parties. Admittedly, the term center is widely, if loosely, used in both journalistic comments and in academic descriptions of the functioning of party systems in individual countries. Nevertheless, European party systems are rarely viewed from a center perspective. On the contrary, the idea of a center finds little favor with scholars. (Daalder, 1984: 92)

The recent literature has shown that there is indeed a renewed interest in the centre, and in the study of centre parties in particular. Regretfully, the problem of conceptual inadequacy still plagues the field, and has affected most of the new research as well.

The adoption of the centre label by an ever-growing number of parties with different ideologies, in quite divergent party systems and throughout the expanding democratic world, is another clear indication that the academic literature requires a reassessment of the centre concept. The collapse of the former Soviet Union has brought about the demise of communist parties in Western Europe, and the movement of such parties away from the extreme left. This development, coupled with the rise of the extreme right in many of these same countries, means that moderate parties on both left and right are being forced to distinguish themselves from the extremists and are being pushed closer to the centre. There appears to be a cross-national pattern exhibited by a mass migration of parties towards the centre – but not necessarily the middle. In order to avoid an inevitable overcrowding of what is already an ill-defined category, clearer boundaries needed to be delineated. This chapter has attempted to achieve this by alerting scholars of party systems to the danger of confusing an objective and universal term with a subjective and contingent one, and by introducing the middle party concept which can move, grow and remain applicable as the space of electoral competition expands or contracts.

This chapter has introduced a clear delineation of what a centre party is, what a centre party is not and a middle party is, what the relevance of the term median party is, what the descriptive attribute of the term pivot party can provide, what the attributes of a central party are and how far the centre label can mislead us, and has.

During the extensive statistical analysis, presented in the following chapter, parties that fall between 4 and 6 on a 10-point, fixed, universal, ideological left–right scale will be considered centre parties; that is, all parties that occupy the metrical centre of a cross-national ideological continuum, or are near it. It is the parliamentary strength of such ideologically positioned centre parties which will be correlated with the level of party system polarization.

Notes

[1.] The core of Daalder's (1984) article is a systematic analysis and critique of the concept of the centre, which needs to be addressed. His first objection is identifying the centre with the median voter. This raises several problems: (a) how voters are to be ranked; (b) how party size will be taken into account; (c) the question of different voting on successive votes; and (d) the shifting of the centre. This study's definition of the centre is not based on voters' perceptions, but on ideological party location. The centre is, therefore, not identified with the median voter, thereby removing Daalder's first criticism. Nonetheless, the specific problems he pointed out still need to be answered: (a) parties are ranked according to expert judgements; (b) party size should be taken into account by the appropriate measurement instruments, such as the one which this study proposes for polarization; (c) parties do change their relative positions *vis-à-vis* the other parties on different votes, but a hierarchy of voting overcomes this. The formation of a government and the vote necessary to confirm it in office subordinate all other votes. Moreover, according to this study's definition, voting is not the essential element. Voting itself is subordinate to the assumed dominant ideological alignments of the party system. Concerning (d), the shifting of the centre, this study does not perceive a problem. Daalder argued that as political coalitions are formed, the centre will shift from the median voter in parliament to the median voter in the coalition. Since this study does not equate the centre with the median voter, no shift takes place when a coalition is formed.

Daalder's second and third sets of criticisms revolve around the left–right continuum and multidimensional space. He objected to the influence of geometric thinking, imposing individual self-locations on the left–right scale, the kind of data and analysis techniques used, and the difference between perceptions and behaviour. Again, most of the problems are overcome when one drops the voter self-perception measurement, while the rest are based on the assumption that reducing a multidimensional universe to a unidimensional ordering is a mistake.

Daalder's last two sets of objections concerned the mechanics of the centre and cleavage analysis. Concerning the former, he countered Sartori's arguments on centripetal and centrifugal competition, stating that both could take place simultaneously. This is not inconsistent with Sartori, who simply stated that in a polarized pluralist party system centrifugal competition will prevail over the centripetal tendencies. Concerning cleavage analysis, Daalder pointed to the dangers inherent in the use of the related terminology, stating that centrist positions are more realistic for some cleavages than for others. This line of argument is quite similar to both Duverger's declared dualistic logic that discounts a centre, and to Stokes' (1963) discussion of 'valence issues' which are non-sequential. Both have been criticized widely, and found to be wanting.

2. Ieraci (1992: 20) defines centre parties as 'governing parties' which 'display or should display high values of coalition and governing potential'. A more correct definition would be pro-system parties. For van Roozendaal (1990) a centre party is actually the 'dominant central player' and includes the possibility of an extreme party being in that position. A more appropriate concept would be that of a central party, i.e. of central relevance, and not a centre party.

3. This is similar to Scully's (1992: 206) mistaken definition of centre parties as those parties that 'lie in between fundamental political alternatives ... by "center" I am not referring to a geometric point equidistant from the poles, but rather an intermediate or in-between "space"'. Thus, what Scully defines as a centre party is actually a middle party according to this study's definition, and what this study defines as a centre party is exactly what Scully said he was not referring to.

4. For an in-depth analysis of pivotal centre parties see Keman (1994).

5. For a discussion concerning the centre in opposing approaches to the Italian party system, see van Loenen (1990) and Hazan (1994).

6. For the sake of illustration, several questionable placements of parties are included. Two examples are as follows: after the break-up of the United Socialist Party (PSU) in 1968, the PSDI is located to the right of the DC (third period), but subsequently returns to its original position; the PR in the late 1970s leap-frogs over the PCI into the middle (fourth period). These placements are based on Marradi (1982).

7. The comparative analysis is made possible by the work begun by the Manifesto Research Group (Budge *et al.*, 1987), which has provided comparative data that can be used for delineating between centre and middle parties. This study adopts their more recent mappings of party systems (Laver and Budge, 1992), in order to illustrate and clarify the concepts advanced in this chapter. Figures 2.2 and 2.3 are thus based on these data.

Part II

The Model

3

Assessing a Relationship

3.1 The Countries

Assessing the relationship between the parliamentary size of centre parties and the level of party system polarization, and thereby testing the research hypothesis, requires the following caveat: the measures must be allowed to vary in order to be studied. That is, the measurement of change at the party system level in terms of the percentage of seats for centre parties and the level of systemic polarization must not be distorted by the existence of biased electoral systems. Thus, this analysis requires and is limited to multiparty democracies using proportional representation electoral systems. It is essentially in such democracies that centre parties exist and, once established, can be relatively confident that electoral gains will not be diminished when translated into parliamentary seats.[1] The absence of the first criterion, a multiparty democracy, in most cases excludes the presence of a centre party; while the absence of the second, a proportional electoral system, will produce poor indicators of either an increase or decrease for both parties and polarization. Therefore, the UK, which uses the 'first-past-the-post' single-member constituency plurality system, and France, which uses the two-ballot majority system, are excluded from the analysis.[2]

The final demarcation concerns the ability to classify parties on the left–right dimension. Both the measures of centre party strength and the level of systemic polarization are based on the relevance and applicability of this scale, which provides a standard against which the measures can be assessed over both time and space. The left–right scale, however, does not seem to apply to the Irish party system. The significance of a left–right dimension is less meaningful in Ireland than in most other Western European countries (Inglehart and Klingemann, 1976: 250–4). The two main parties compete primarily along a nationalist–constitutional cleavage and lack any relevant left–right ideological differences (Carty, 1981; Gallagher, 1981). According to Budge and Farlie (1983: 55), 'The ethos of [the Irish] party system diverges from the general spirit of socialist-bourgeois party competition.' Ireland is, therefore, to be seen as a deviant case in terms of the applicability and relevance of a left–right scale, and will not be considered.[3]

When the above limitations to the number of countries are taken into account,[4] we are left with the following Western European parliamentary democracies: Austria, Belgium, Denmark, Finland, Italy, The Netherlands, Norway, Spain, Sweden and Germany.[5] The time-frame of the cross-national analysis in this part covers the period between 1979 and 1989.

3.2   The Measures

The level of party system polarization, based on the parliamentary strengths of parties, was assessed for each national election during the 1979–89 period, thereby providing at least three scores of polarization for each country in Table 3.1. Some countries have four or five polarization scores, depending on the frequency of elections during the 1980s.

The pattern that immediately reveals itself is that, other than the few outliers, there is a very limited variation in the polarization scores,[6] exhibiting a relatively uniform and stable level of European polarization.[7] An overwhelming majority of the cases (89 per cent) are clustered between the polarization scores of 3.14 and 5.23. That is, almost 90 per cent of the cases are concentrated within less than 10 per cent of the scale's potential variation.[8] This pattern exhibits a close clustering around a mean of 4.23, with a standard deviation of 0.960, which is similar to both the mode and the median, thereby producing roughly a normal distribution (Figure 3.1).

Another feature of the polarization index is that some of the countries fail to correspond to the generally perceived level of party system polarization. Italy, for example, is usually considered to have a highly polarized party system. According to this scale it is ranked in the middle of the list of countries based on average systemic polarization between 1979 and 1989 (4.44) – surpassed by Sweden (4.47), The Netherlands (4.55), Spain (4.78) and Norway (5.87) – and is close to the Western

European overall average. This is a function of the polarization index, which both uses a weighted mean and also weights each party's position for every national election, thereby assessing polarization in a much more precise manner than a non-weighted measure.[9]

The reason for weighting each party can be elaborated by discussing why the polarization score for Italy is not exceptionally high. During the 1980s, the Italian party system had two major parties: the Italian Communist Party (PCI) located at 1.6 on the 10-point left–right scale, which averaged over 30 per cent of the seats; and the Christian Democrats (DC) centrally located at 5.4 on the left–right scale, averaging over 38 percent. The third largest party in Italy was scarcely one-half the size

Table 3.1 European polarization scores, 1979–89

Country	Year	Polarization
Austria	1979	2.19
	1983	2.20
	1986	2.39
Belgium	1981	4.27
	1985	3.94
	1987	4.18
Denmark	1979	4.41
	1981	4.54
	1984	4.29
	1987	4.16
	1988	4.44
Finland	1979	4.09
	1983	3.69
	1987	3.45
Italy	1979	4.31
	1983	4.73
	1987	4.29
Netherlands	1981	4.50
	1982	5.21
	1986	4.09
	1989	4.39
Norway	1981	5.18
	1985	5.10
	1989	7.34
Spain	1979	3.69
	1982	5.04
	1986	5.15
	1989	5.23
Sweden	1979	4.33
	1982	4.72
	1985	4.37
	1988	4.16
Germany	1980	3.14
	1983	3.36
	1987	3.33

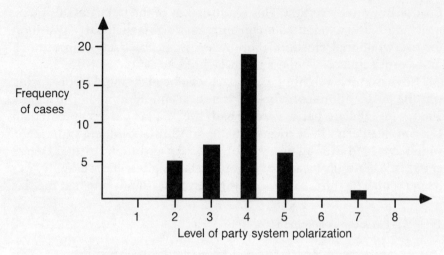

Figure 3.1 Polarization histogram

of either of these two major parties, and was positioned between them – the Italian Socialist Party (PSI) located at 3.1 on the left–right scale. There was no large party anywhere to the right of the DC, or to the left of the PCI. The centre of gravity of the Italian party system, therefore, lay between the PCI and the DC – that is, between 1.6 and 5.4 respectively. Yet the Italian party system possessed an extreme left party, Proletarian Democracy (DP), located at 0.5 on the left–right scale, and an extreme right party, the Italian Socialist Movement (MSI), located at 9.1 on the same scale. These parties were, however, electorally weak. DP hovered under 2 per cent during the 1980s, while the MSI fluctuated around 6 per cent. If one simply measured the distance between the two most extreme parties (9.1 − 0.5 = 8.6), the Italian party system would indeed appear to have been highly polarized. Even if one argues that DP was irrelevant, the distance between the MSI and the next most extreme left party, the PCI, is still a very high 7.5. Therefore, entering parties such as DP or the MSI as non-weighted equals to the PCI and the DC will lead to an exaggerated measure of polarization, lacking any empirical or theoretical justification. In the words of Bartolini and Mair:

> it is inconceivable that the distance separating two small parties will have the same impact . . . as that separating two large parties, and in this sense, the 'leftness' [i.e. position along the left–right scale] of a small party in a policy space cannot be considered to have the same impact . . . as the 'leftness' of a large party in the same position. (Bartolini and Mair, 1990: 11)

The rank-ordering of countries according to polarization in this study corresponds to the conventional ordering of states in terms of ideological polarization, but the clustering around a moderate mean produced by this study's weighted measure of polarization is intended to capture the true distance among parties by tapping their political strengths. Omitting this variable of political weight – thereby obtaining non-weighted measures of party system polarization – would give exaggerated value to extreme parties, generate a biased polarization score and produce invalid relationships between polarization and other systemic variables.

The weighted measure of polarization also facilitates the assessment of party system polarization in another fashion – there is no need to decide which parties are relevant and which are not. Sartori's (1976: 121–5) criteria, for example, of which parties are to be counted as relevant can be summarized as all parties that possess either coalition or blackmail potential. Coalition potential includes all ideologically acceptable coalition partners, i.e. all pro-system parties. Blackmail potential applies to all ideologically unacceptable parties that are strong enough to affect competition, i.e. all large anti-system parties. Thus, only small extremist parties are disqualified for a lack of relevance by Sartori. This study's measure of polarization is affected only negligibly even when these minor and irrelevant parties are included, due to its weighted nature. There is, therefore, no need to embark on a painstaking evaluation of every party system in order to assess the qualifications of relevance for its parties. Moreover, this task is often counter-productive, because it is exactly the judgement over relevance that encounters the harshest criticism. The weighted measurement of polarization adopted here avoids the need for what is inherently a biased assessment, and thereby removes one of the major targets of fault.

This point can be clearly illustrated if we look at the 1983 election results of two very different party systems: the extreme multipartism of Italy and the essential two-partism of Great Britain. In both countries more than five parties won seats in the lower house of parliament. How would an assessment of party relevance impact this study's measure of polarization for each country? Table 3.2 suggests that the answer is very little. The total change in the polarization score for Italy was less than 4 per cent of the original score after all of the potentially irrelevant parties were excluded. For Britain the change was less than 2 per cent, and this is further reduced to less than 1 per cent when all but the two main parties are disqualified for lack of relevance.

The second major variable in this study is the size of the centre party

Table 3.2 Polarization scores and party relevance

Country election	Relevant parties	Irrelevant parties	Polarization
Italy 1983	DC, PCI, PSI, MSI, PRI, PSDI, PLI, PR, DP	None	4.73
Italy 1983	DC, PCI, PSI, MSI, PRI, PSDI, PLI, PR	DP	4.59
Italy 1983	DC, PCI, PSI, MSI, PRI, PSDI, PLI	DP, PR	4.55
Britain 1983	CON, LAB, LIB/SDP, SNP, PC, UU	None	6.58
Britain 1983	CON, LAB, LIB/SDP	SNP, PC, UU	6.45
Britain 1983	CON, LAB	LIB/SDP, SNP, PC, UU	6.52

DC, Christian Democrats; PCI, Italian Communist Party; PSI, Italian Socialist Party; MSI, Italian Socialist Movement; PRI, Italian Republican Party; PSDI, Italian Social Democratic Party; PLI, Italian Liberal Party; PR, Radical Party; DP, Proletarian Democracy; CON, Conservatives; LAB, Labour; LIB/SDP, Liberals/Social Democrats; SNP, Scottish Nationalists; PC, Plaid Cymru; UU, Ulster Unionists

or parties. This measure is much less complicated. Based on the previously adopted 10-point left–right scale, produced by Castles and Mair (1984), the original 10 points have been collapsed into the five categories presented in Table 3.3.[10]

The size of the centre is simply the percentage of seats won by all parties who fall between 4 and 6 on the scale, for each specific national election. In other words, the measure of parties of the centre captures those parties which occupy the metrical centre area of a cross-national, competitive ideological continuum (see Chapter 2).

By collapsing the 10-point left–right scale into five party groups, and adopting a specific computation of party positions, it is possible to assess not only the size of the centre, but also the sizes of the moderate right, the moderate left, the extreme right and the extreme left. Figure 3.2 presents the average party category's parliamentary strength for the countries included in this study, by consolidating the moderate left and the moderate right into a single category of moderate parties, and doing the same for the extreme left and extreme right into a category of extreme parties.[11]

Table 3.3 Left–right categories

Category	Range
Extreme left	0–1.9
Moderate left	2.0–3.9
Centre	4.0–6.0
Moderate right	6.1–8.0
Extreme right	8.1–10

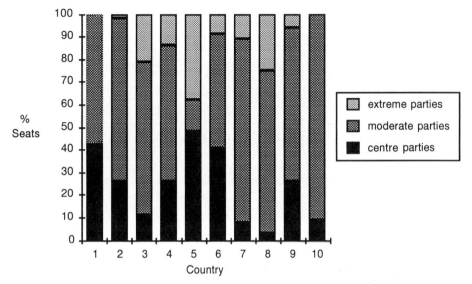

1 = Austria; 2 = Belgium; 3 = Denmark; 4 = Finland; 5 = Italy;
6 = The Netherlands; 7 = Norway; 8 = Spain; 9 = Sweden; 10 = Germany

Figure 3.2 Moderate, centre and extreme parties by country

3.3   The Results

Aggregate election data, together with the measures elaborated above, allow for statistical testing of the hypothesized relationship between the parliamentary size of the centre and the level of party system polarization.[12] The result of this first test is a negative correlation. Across all 35 cases, the correlation between the centre's share of parliamentary seats and the level of party system polarization is: $r = -0.354$.[13] Being negative, it is quite contrary to Sartori's theory, and seems to support Duverger's. It appears that the centre is indeed a moderating element. That is, as we move from left to right across the cases in the scatterplot (Figure 3.3), the size of the centre parties grows and there is a clear linear decline in the level of systemic polarization. The theory relating the growth of the centre to increased polarization finds no support whatsoever.

However, if we take another look at the scatterplot of results presented in Figure 3.3, it is clear that there is one outlier in the upper left-hand corner, and outliers in the bottom right-hand corner. The remaining 31 cases are all scattered across a rather thin band of polarization between 3.14 and 5.23, while the centre parties share of parliamentary seats ranges from less than 5 per cent to almost 50 per cent.

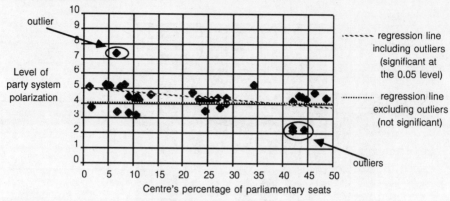

Figure 3.3 Size of centre parties with level of polarization in Europe, 1979–89
(scatterplot of all 35 national cases)

These outliers could be deviant national cases obscuring what is essentially a horizontal clustering,[14] signifying no relationship at all. The location of the outliers in opposite corners of the scatterplot could be the driving force behind the negative correlation.

Indeed, once the outliers are excluded, any relationship between the centre parties' share of seats and systemic polarization disappears. The correlation goes down drastically from $r = -0.354$ to $r = -0.019$ and becomes statistically insignificant.[15] The previously significant negative correlation was, therefore, driven entirely by the few outliers.

This revised analysis allows for a re-evaluation of the assumed relationship. The expected association between the parliamentary growth of the centre parties and the level of party system polarization, negative or positive, has *not* been found.

3.4   Interpreting the Ambiguous Findings

Why should this be so? Why should the real association not conform to either of the two ostensibly plausible, yet opposite explanations of the centre parties' impact on polarization, as advanced by Sartori and Duverger? Could there be a non-linear pattern that the measures are not designed to pick up? Might there be a trend taking place which newly created measures would uncover? Or could the measures themselves be hiding the relationship being analysed? The answer appears to be all of the above.

The assumption that was introduced into the regression analysis affects the measure of polarization by generating polarization scores which are not objective. The assumption is that the centre parties' share of parliamentary seats is growing. In other words, as we travel from left to right on the *x*-axis of the scatterplot, the centre parties' share grows ten-fold from less than 5 per cent to almost 50 per cent of the seats in parliament. With the assumption that the parliamentary strength of the centre parties is expanding, the measure of party system polarization is now inclined to decrease. That is, as we move from those cases where the centre is relatively small to those where it is large, the centre parties' percentage of parliamentary seats grows, and consequently the non-centre parties' share of seats diminishes, thereby causing the centre parties to weigh more in the measure of polarization and produce a mitigating score. In short, the measure of polarization is predisposed to decline as the centre parties grow. Therefore, the relationship between the parliamentary size of the centre parties and the level of party system polarization is expected to be negative – as the centre parties' share of seats grows, the level of systemic polarization diminishes.

This is not, however, the result obtained. The initial negative correlation was found to be a function of the outliers; but once they were eliminated, there appeared to be no relationship at all. The scatterplot clearly shows a horizontal clustering, not a negative slope from the left-hand corner down to the right-hand corner. This can be interpreted in only one way: as we move along the scatterplot from those countries with minor centre parties to those with medium and major ones, the level of party system polarization is maintained within a relatively constant cluster. How could this be? If the parties of the centre are increasing their share of seats, but the level of party system polarization remains constant, there must be an additional trend offsetting the growth of the centre parties which counters the polarization measure's proclivity to decrease.

An exploration of two hypothetical explanations and the elaboration of a model for this second and neutralizing pattern are presented in Chapter 4. Chapters 5 and 6 provide an empirical test of the hypothesized explanations.

Notes

[1.] It is generally believed that single-member constituency plurality electoral systems penalize parties by as much as cubic proportions (Kendall and Stuart, 1950). Rae (1967) has argued that the difference of the mean bonuses awarded under the plurality formula in comparison to the proportional formula is a six-fold difference. A clear example of this distortion is the 1983 election in the UK. The Labour Party won 27.6 per cent of the national vote and 32.2 per cent of the parliamentary seats, while the Liberal/Social Democratic Alliance won just 2.2 per cent less of the national vote (25.4 per cent) but received only 3.5 per cent of the seats. With a relative Labour advantage over the Alliance of just 8 per cent of the vote, the electoral system translated this into a relative advantage of more than 800 per cent of the seats.

2. Statistical support for excluding the UK and France from this analysis is given in Note 13.

3. Statistical support for Ireland's exclusion is provided in Note 13.

4. Only those countries for which left–right party positions appear in the Castles and Mair (1984) index are included. Adding additional countries – even if replicating the 'expert' ranking were possible – would be inconsistent with the continuum produced in 1984, due to the seminal changes which have taken place in Europe.

5. The Federal Republic of Germany, which was distinct from the German Democratic Republic during the entire period of the research.

6. All three Austrian elections are deviantly low on the polarization index, while the Norwegian election of 1989 provides the single deviant high polarization score.

7. These polarization scores have been correlated with other polarization indexes from the literature, with the following results:

Polarization index	r	R^2	Sigma T	N
Sigelman and Yough	0.601	0.361	0.05	11
Ersson and Lane	0.757	0.573	0.01	13

Sigelman and Yough's (1978) measures were based on the decade of the 1960s, and Ersson and Lane's (1982) measure was based on the post-1945 period (in this regression test, polarization scores for countries omitted from the research were computed and included, i.e. Great Britain, France, and Ireland).

8. The possible range for the polarization scale is from 0, when one party wins 100 per cent of the seats, to 25, when two parties each win 50 per cent of the seats and are at the maximum distance from each other on the left–right scale – one at 0 and the other at 10.

9. The values for the average weighted means generated by this study's measure of polarization for the 1980s have been correlated against the weighted means used by Sigelman and Yough (1978) for the 1960s; the result is: $r = 0.841$; $R^2 = 0.708$; significant at the 0.01 level ($N = 11$). The utilization of weighted measures means that each party's position along the left–right scale is multiplied by its share of seats. Parties on the threshold of a majority will therefore have a stronger impact on the measures than those on the verge of extinction, thereby producing more accurate results. The relevance and advantage of weighted measures of party strength for spatial analysis have been advocated by Bartolini and Mair (1990: 11–12).

10. Castles and Mair (1984) divided their 10-point left–right scale with smaller spaces allocated to the extremes than to the moderates and centre as follows: 0–1.25, ultra-left; 1.25–3.75, moderate left; 3.75–6.25, centre; 6.25–8.75, moderate right; 8.75–10, ultra-right. Their division resulted in parties such as the Communist Party (KPB/PCB) in Belgium, the Socialist People's Party (SF) and the Progress Party (FRP) in Denmark, the Communist Party (PCF) in France, the Communist Party (DKP) in Germany, the Communist Party (PCI) in Italy and the Radical Political

Party (PPR) in The Netherlands all being classified as moderate parties, and not extremist parties, which would be more appropriate. The division in this study allows each category to encompass a similar amount of space on the continuum and reduces the number of misclassified parties.

11. The averages for each category over the national elections between 1979 and 1989 have been adjusted to sum to 100 per cent.

12. The statistical correlations run throughout this and subsequent chapters are based on cross-sectional analysis, as are the results. An increase, or decrease, in percentage of parliamentary seats, or level of polarization, does not take place within any specific country but is inferred from the cross-sectional data based on particular cases which are brought together for the purpose of statistical analysis. Overall patterns exhibited by the data will be used to produce generalizations concerning the relationship between centre parties and systemic polarization, as well as between centre parties and other parties. Whenever terminology referring to party growth is not qualified by a reference to cross-sectional data, the reason is simply the attempt to avoid repetitive and tortured prose, rather than to negate the existence of developmental patterns.

13. $R^2 = 0.125$; $b = -0.022$; significant at the 0.05 level.
Statistical support for the exclusion of the UK, France and Ireland from this study is now provided by the regression analysis:

(a) In the case of the UK and France, the absence of a proportional representation electoral system distorts the results at the party system level and would serve a better indicator of the influence that the electoral system has on the level of polarization in the party system than the impact that the size of centre parties might have. When the UK and France are included along with the other cases, the relationship between the size of centre parties and the level of party system polarization loses all significance due to the distinctiveness of these two countries. To resolve this problem, all the cases' centre scores were entered, while the UK and France were included as a dummy variable, and a regression was run with polarization. The results show a clear relationship with polarization: $r = 0.598$; $R^2 = 0.372$; $b = 3.069$; significant at the 0.01 level. That is, the UK and France have a substantial impact on polarization above and beyond, or even independent of, their centre score. Due to this obscuring impact, they have been omitted.

(b) Statistically, Ireland's distinctiveness also has an obscuring impact on the relationship between the centre and polarization. When this distinctiveness is filtered, and Ireland is run as a dummy variable (having omitted the UK and France already), the difference remains influential ($r = -0.753$; $R^2 = 0.621$; $b = -3.584$; significant at the 0.01 level), making Ireland a candidate for exclusion as well. Furthermore, Ireland's use of the single transferable vote electoral system could support its omission from this study for similar reasons as were used to justify excluding the UK and France.

(c) When these three countries are included, a regression assumption, heteroskedasticity, is violated. When they are excluded, the data are homoskedastic. Moreover, when these countries are included, and the squared residual between the independent and dependent variables is correlated with the independent variable, the result is -0.494, thereby exhibiting a non-random residual pattern. When these countries are excluded, the squared residual is reduced to −0.025 and becomes almost entirely random. The large difference between these scores is also an indication that the deviant cases, i.e. outliers, from a linear pattern are to be found at the extremes, exactly where the UK, France and Ireland would have appeared on the scatterplot, providing a further reason for omitting these countries from the research.

14. The distinctiveness of these outlying cases – already apparent from Table 3.1 – which obscures the real relationship evident in the scatterplot is proven by including them as dummy variables. When the dummy variable of the outlying high polarization case (Norway in 1989) is included as an additional variable in a multiple regression, the result is: $r = 0.689$; $b = 3.010$; $R^2 = 0.475$; significant at the 0.01 level. When the dummy variable of the outlying low polarization scores (Austria 1979, 1983, 1986) is included as an additional variable in a multiple regression, the result is: $r = -0.736$; $b = -2.039$; $R^2 = 0.541$; significant at the 0.01 level. Since there is no theoretical justification for excluding these cases – unlike the UK, France and Ireland – they will be maintained throughout the research, but their distinctiveness will be filtered when necessary.

15. $R^2 = 0.00$; $b = 0.00$; significant $t = 0.918$.

4

Generating a Model

4.1 Hypothesizing a Relationship

The adoption of the three-fold party categorization – dividing the left–right continuum into centre, moderate and extreme parties – allows for two plausible theoretical explanations of how the centre parties' share of parliamentary seats grows while the level of systemic polarization remains constant. The first concentrates on the movement of voter support, and hence parliamentary seats, from one category to the next. The second focuses on a shift of parties along the left–right scale, possibly in response to such a movement of voter support.

If it is assumed that the centre parties are growing – moving from left to right along the cases in the scatterplot (Figure 3.3) – then at least one of the other two categories must decrease. Without at least one category losing parliamentary seats, there would be no seats available to be gained by one or both of the other categories. The question is, which combination of gains versus losses for each category produces a stable level of polarization?

If it is the extreme parties who are on the losing end, then we should see a clear decline in the level of party system polarization, whether it is both centre and moderate parties who gain seats from the extreme parties, or the centre parties alone while the moderate parties are held constant. In Example 1 (Table 4.1) both centre and moderate parties gain seats from the extreme parties – the classical case of depolarization. The results show a dramatic decline in the level of systemic polarization.[1]

In Example 2 (Table 4.2), the centre parties alone grow, at the expense of the extreme parties, while the moderate parties remain

Table 4.1 Example 1

Election	1	2	3
Centre parties	15	25	35
Moderate parties	50	55	60
Extreme parties	35	20	5
Polarization	7.6	5.4	3.2

Table 4.2 Example 2

Election	1	2	3
Centre parties	15	25	35
Moderate parties	65	65	65
Extreme parties	20	10	0
Polarization	5.8	4.2	2.6

constant. The result is an even sharper decline in the level of polarization.

This does not explain the lack of a decrease in the level of polarization exhibited by the scatterplot in Figure 3.3. If it is not the extreme parties who are losing seats while the centre parties grow – regardless of whether the moderate parties also gain or remain constant – then it must be the moderate parties who are on the losing side. A second theoretical assumption can, therefore, be introduced: the moderate parties are losing seats. That is, not only are the centre parties growing – the first theoretical assumption – but at the same time the moderate parties are diminishing. There are now only three remaining possibilities: (1) moderate and extreme parties are both losing seats; (2) moderate parties lose seats while extreme parties remain constant; or (3) moderate parties lose seats but extreme parties win seats.

Table 4.3 Example 3

Election	1	2	3
Centre parties	15	25	35
Moderate parties	65	60	55
Extreme parties	20	15	10
Polarization	5.8	4.8	3.8

Table 4.4 Example 4

Election	1	2	3
Centre parties	15	25	35
Moderate parties	65	55	45
Extreme parties	20	20	20
Polarization	5.8	5.4	5.0

In Example 3 (Table 4.3) the centre parties are growing at the expense of both moderate and extreme parties – another classical case of depolarization. The result is, as expected, a declining level of party system polarization. The first possibility is therefore rejected; as the moderate parties lose seats, the extreme parties cannot decline simultaneously if systemic polarization is to remain relatively constant.

Now the question is: who are the moderate parties losing seats to? Do the centre parties gain all the lost moderate parties' seats, leaving the extreme parties unchanged? Or are the moderate parties' seats lost to both centre and extreme parties? In Example 4 (Table 4.4) the centre parties grow at the expense of the moderate parties, while the extreme parties remain unchanged. The result, once again, is a decrease in the level of polarization. However, the decrease is rather slight.

What would happen if the loss of the moderate parties did not go entirely to the centre parties? In Example 5 (Table 4.5) the moderate parties are losing seats to both centre and extreme parties. We have here the only example in which the level of party system polarization does not decrease, but actually increases, even though the extreme parties won only one-half the amount of additional seats gained by the centre parties.[2] All other possible combinations produce decreasing levels of systemic polarization.

Thus, if the centre's growth is the basic assumption, then two conclusions emerge: (1) the level of party system polarization can increase only when both the extreme parties and the centre parties profit from

Table 4.5 Example 5

Election	1	2	3
Centre parties	15	25	35
Moderate parties	80	65	50
Extreme parties	5	10	15
Polarization	4.0	4.2	4.4

the loss of the moderate parties' seats, but at different rates; and (2) the level of polarization can remain relatively constant if the extreme parties grow at a substantially lesser rate than the proportion of new seats gained by the centre parties. A third theoretical assumption can now be entered: the extreme parties are gaining seats. Not only are the centre parties growing and the moderate parties diminishing, but the extreme parties are on the winning end as well.

In summary, the theoretical argument is: if the parliamentary shares of seats for both the centre parties and the extreme parties grow simultaneously, at the expense of the moderate parties, then, and only then, would the level of party system polarization remain constant. Have we uncovered the trend that the measures were hiding which can explain why systemic polarization did not decline even though the centre parties' share of seats grew ten-fold? In order to show this, empirical evidence must be provided showing that both centre and extreme parties profited from a decline of the moderate parties. This task will be attempted in the following chapter.

However, could there also be a second possible theoretical explanation which can account for the unvarying pattern of systemic polarization, despite the rising parliamentary strength of the centre parties? In building the previous explanation, each of the three categories in Examples 1 to 5 was located at the middle of its range on the 10-point, left–right scale without being allowed to vary.[3] Would allowing the categories to move within their range on the left–right scale, while the centre category increased its share of parliamentary seats, produce a plausible alternative theoretical explanation?

4.2   An Alternative Relationship

The classical scenario for a decline in the level of systemic polarization would be one in which both extreme and moderate parties lose, while the centre parties gain, parliamentary seats. Such a clear centripetal pattern is a pure example of depolarization, as shown previously in Example 3 (Table 4.3). But would this also be true if the locations of both moderate and extreme parties did not remain stable, e.g. if the moderate parties felt as though the centre ground was no longer open to competition and decided to move towards the far ends of their range, locating themselves closer to the extreme parties and pushing them to compete further out as well?

Example 6, in Table 4.6, shows the moderate parties moving outwards at each election: the moderate right parties move from 6.5 to 7.0

Table 4.6 Example 6

Election	1		2		3	
	L-R	%	L-R	%	L-R	%
Centre parties	5.0	15	5.0	25	5.0	35
Moderate right parties	6.5	33	7.0	30	7.5	28
Moderate left parties	3.5	32	3.0	30	2.5	27
Extreme right parties	8.5	10	9.0	8	9.5	5
Extreme left parties	1.5	10	1.0	7	0.5	5
Polarization	3.9		4.8		5.5	

and then to 7.5; while the moderate left parties move from 3.5 to 3.0 and finally to 2.5. The extreme parties move in a similar pattern. During these outward moves, both moderate and extreme parties are losing parliamentary seats to the centre parties (which in Example 3 produced a drastic decline in polarization). The resulting polarization scores, however, show an increase in the level of party system polarization. This means that the centrifugal movement of the moderate parties and the extreme parties, despite their loss of seats, was enough to counter and overcome the centripetal movement of voters. In short, allowing parties to move along the left–right scale can impact decisively on the level of systemic polarization.

Example 6 assumed that both moderate and extreme parties moved centrifugally. Would the results change if only the moderate parties adopted such a strategy? In such a scenario the centre parties are growing and driving the moderate parties away from the now occupied central arena, but the extreme parties do not move out as well, preferring to hold their positions and combat the outward-moving moderate parties.

In Example 7 (Table 4.7) the moderate parties move in the same

Table 4.7 Example 7

Election	1		2		3	
	L-R	%	L-R	%	L-R	%
Centre parties	5.0	15	5.0	25	5.0	35
Moderate right parties	6.5	33	7.0	28	7.5	23
Moderate left parties	3.5	32	3.0	27	2.5	22
Extreme right parties	9.0	10	9.0	10	9.0	10
Extreme left parties	1.0	10	1.0	10	1.0	10
Polarization	4.7		5.4		6.0	

Table 4.8 Example 8

Election	1		2		3	
	L-R	%	L-R	%	L-R	%
Centre parties	5.0	15	5.0	25	5.0	35
Moderate right parties	6.5	33	7.0	30	7.5	28
Moderate left parties	3.5	32	3.0	30	2.5	27
Extreme right parties	9.0	10	9.0	8	9.0	5
Extreme left parties	1.0	10	1.0	7	1.0	5
Polarization	4.7		4.8		5.0	

manner as they did in Example 6, and lose seats. However, the extreme parties do not move and are able to maintain their shares of seats. This means that all of the seats changing hands are moving inwards from moderate to centre parties – what should be a clear case of depolarization, as shown previously in Example 4. However, the movement of the moderate parties away from the centre, despite their declining parliamentary strength, is enough to produce a rising polarization score.

One additional example can make the importance of this pattern even clearer. If both moderate and extreme parties decline in parliamentary strength, while only the moderate parties move outwards, will the level of systemic polarization still show an increase? Example 8 (Table 4.8) shows a decline in the share of both moderate and extreme seats, thereby exhibiting a centripetal electoral pattern that covers the entire system. The extreme parties lose seats and do not move from their location on the left–right scale, while the moderate parties lose seats and move away from the growing centre. The result is an almost constant, but still slightly rising, level of party system polarization.

This means that a second theoretical explanation can be presented. If there appears to be no relationship, or even a negative relationship, between the parliamentary strengths of the centre and those of the extreme parties – should the empirical evidence provide no support for the first theoretical explanation – then party movement along the left–right scale could be the reason for the rather constant level of polarization as the centre parties increase their share of parliamentary seats. In other words, if it cannot be shown that the decline of the moderate parties produces parliamentary gains for both centre and extreme parties, then the unchanging level of systemic polarization can still be explained. As the centre parties grow, they push the moderate parties to compete for votes further from the centre, and this centrifugal movement by the moderate parties is enough to offset the declining level of party system polarization which the centripetal movement of voters should have produced. If the extreme parties also adopt a centrifugal strategy this pattern will be exacerbated.

In summary, two theoretical explanations have been uncovered for the trend that the measures were hiding. As we move from left to right across the scatterplot of cases presented in Figure 3.3, for the level of systemic polarization to remain relatively constant across almost 90 per cent of these cases, even though the centre parties increase their share from 5 per cent to 50 per cent of the parliamentary seats, either: (1) the extreme parties must be profiting as well; or (2) there must be a centrifugal movement of parties along the left–right scale. If either of the hypotheses is validated empirically, this would provide substantial support for Sartori's theoretical framework concerning the impact that centre parties have on party competition. Whether the growth of the centre parties is positively related to a growth of the extreme parties, or to a centrifugal movement of parties, the result appears to be centre-driven polarization which suppresses the moderating impact of the centre parties' growth.

Now that we know what the underlying pattern might be, it is both necessary and compelling to analyse the empirical data once again in order to assess whether or not either of these trends actually exists. The first theoretical explanation is empirically tested in Chapter 5, while an examination of the second explanation is provided in Chapter 6.

Notes

[1] The figures used in this and subsequent examples are the percentages of seats won. Although both moderate and extreme parties are collapsed in the examples for the sake of presentation, they are maintained in their original separate categories for the measurement of polarization. That is, a moderate parties' score of 50 per cent of the seats is composed of 25 per cent for the moderate right parties and 25 per cent for the moderate left parties, and likewise for extreme right and extreme left parties. Each category is located at the middle of its range on the 10-point left–right scale: extreme right = 9; moderate right = 7; centre = 5; moderate left = 3; extreme left = 1.

[2] Ostensibly we have now switched from a unimodal or bimodal distribution of the party system to a trimodal distribution.

[3] See Note 1.

5

Testing Movement of Voter Support

5.1 Demonstrating Non-linearity

In order to accept the first underlying theoretical relationship between the centre parties' share of parliamentary seats and the level of party system polarization, as elaborated in Chapter 4, it must be shown that as we move from left to right along the scatterplot in Figure 3.3 – i.e. from small to large centre parties – two simultaneous trends take place: moderate parties decrease and extreme parties increase their respective shares of parliamentary seats. Using regression analysis the existence of these two trends can be confirmed if two negative correlations are uncovered: one between centre and moderate parties, and the second between moderate and extreme parties. The regression analysis indeed produces these two negative correlations.

When the parliamentary strength of the centre parties is regressed against that of the moderate parties the result is $r = -0.793$,[1] thereby substantiating the assumption that in those cases where the centre parties increase their share of parliamentary seats, the moderate parties' share declines. When the moderate parties are regressed against the extreme parties, the result is similar ($r = -0.694$),[2] supporting the finding that in those cases where the moderate parties' share of seats declines, the extreme parties profit from this loss. When a multiple regression is run with both independent variables simultaneously – the parliamentary strength of the moderate parties being the dependent variable – the results corroborate those obtained by the previous two bivariate regressions: for the centre, $R = -0.606$; for the extremes, $R = -0.719$.[3] Can we then conclude that there is a positive relationship between centre and extreme parties – that in those cases where the centre parties increase their share of parliamentary seats, the extreme parties will do the same? A multiple regression similar to the one above, but with the centre as the dependent variable, leads to a negative result. The centre has a strongly significant negative relationship to both the moderate parties, $R = -1.366$, and the extreme parties, $R = -0.827$.[4] Yet the answer is not so clear.

When the moderate parties are eliminated, and we return to bivariate correlations, regressing the parliamentary strength of the centre parties against that of the extreme parties results in $r = 0.121$, but it is statistically insignificant.[5] This means not only that centre parties have hardly any impact on extreme parties, but that only 1 per cent of the variance in the size of the extremes is 'explained' by the centre. Should it be assumed that – despite the previous findings which show that in those cases where the parliamentary strength of the moderate parties declines, this produces an increase in both centre and extreme party strength – there is no relationship between centre and extreme parties? Or is this relationship non-linear and the regression equation fails to pick this up? We can begin to find the answer by examining a scatterplot of the parliamentary strengths of extreme and centre parties, presented in Figure 5.1.

Although the plot does not show a clear pattern, it does appear that a 'U'-shaped curve is present. In order to better assess the existence of such a pattern, a variable of the share of centre party parliamentary seats squared, with the origin at the base of the 'U'-shaped curve, was computed and regressed against the extreme parties' share of seats.[6] The results provide proof that a 'U'-shaped pattern indeed exists:

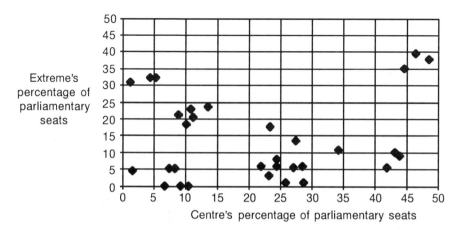

Figure 5.1 Extreme parties with centre parties

$r = 0.517.$[7] This is an improvement over the insignificant linear correlation found between centre and extreme parties.

A description of the relationship uncovered between centre and extreme parties depends on how one divides the centre parties into categories. If a three-fold categorization based on the centre parties' parliamentary share of seats is adopted, then the relationship is non-linear and goes through three phases: (1) a negative one at first; (2) then a levelling-off; and finally (3) a positive relationship. If a dichotomous categorization of the centre parties' parliamentary strength is used, then the relationship between centre and extreme parties exhibits only two phases: a negative trend which is then reversed to a positive trend – two contradicting linear relationships.

The dividing points for the three-fold categorization, based on the centre parties' share of parliamentary seats, appear to be: 0–15 per cent; 15–30 per cent; and 30–50 per cent. It is interesting to note that this is consistent with the three apparent clusters of cases in the first scatter-plot of the parliamentary strength of the centre parties with the level of party system polarization (Figure 3.3). The dividing point for the dichotomous categorization is 20 per cent. This cut-off point is consistent with the two apparent clusters of cases on opposite sides of the parabola deduced from the scatterplot of centre and extreme parties' seats (Figure 5.1). The centre will, therefore, be divided into both two and three categories, as presented in Table 5.1.

Table 5.1 Categories of centre parties (based on percentage of parliamentary seats)

	Three-fold categorization			Dichotomous categorization	
No.	Size	Index	No.	Size	Index
1	Minor	Between 1% and 15%	1	Small	Between 1% and 20%
2	Medium	Between 16% and 30%	2	Large	Between 21% and 49%
3	Major	Between 31% and 49%			

The first, three-fold categorization presents a centre that can be either:

1. a minor party or group of parties, a small coalition partner (i.e. the Radical Liberals, Centre Democrats, and Christian People's Party in Denmark);
2. a medium-sized party or group of parties, an important coalition partner (i.e. the Centre Party and People's Party in Sweden);

3. the major party or group of parties, a necessary and even dominant coalition partner (i.e. the Christian Democratic Appeal and Democrats '66 in The Netherlands).

The dichotomization of the centre cuts through the second category of the three-fold categorization, but since there are no cases of centre parties with 15–20 per cent of the parliamentary seats, it simply merges the second and third categories into a single category. In other words, the centre can be either small and minor, or large and important.

An interesting finding immediately appears as a byproduct of these categorizations. One would expect the sizes of centre parties to vary over time in each country, due to the volatility of the centre's voters, so that one country would not be confined to one category and could be found in two or even all three categories. In fact, not one of the countries in this study has even one election that deviates from a particular category between 1979 and 1989. The three-fold and the dichotomous categorizations are, therefore, mutually exclusive. The result is that countries can be categorized according to the parliamentary size of their centre parties, as presented in Table 5.2.

In order to further assess the relationship between the level of party system polarization and the parliamentary strength of centre parties, two methods are adopted: (1) in accordance with the three-fold categorization of the centre, the difference in mean values for both moderate and extreme parties, as well as for polarization, will be examined; (2) in accordance with the dichotomous categorization of the centre, the correlation coefficients for centre parties against both moderate and extreme parties will be assessed. In other words, based on the three

Table 5.2 Categories of countries (based on centre parties)

Three-fold categorization		Dichotomous categorization	
Centre	Country	Centre	Country
Minor	Denmark Norway Spain Germany	Small	Denmark Norway Spain Germany
Medium	Belgium Finland Sweden	Large	Belgium Finland Sweden Austria
Major	Austria Italy Netherlands		Italy Netherlands

clusters of cases in Figure 3.3 – minor, medium and major centre parties – a three-fold breakdown of means will be used to test for the presence and characteristics of non-linear relationships between the parliamentary strength of centre parties and systemic polarization. This will then be followed by a dichotomous regression analysis, based on the two clusters of cases on either side of the axis of symmetry in Figure 5.1 – small and large centre parties – to ascertain if there exists a linear relationship between the parliamentary strength of centre parties and systemic polarization within either of these two clusters.

5.2 Trichotomous Analysis

When looking at the mean level of polarization,[8] according to the three categories of the centre, we obtain a non-linear pattern, presented graphically in Figure 5.2.

This figure substantiates the preliminary conclusion that there is no linear relationship between the centre parties' share of parliamentary seats and the level of party system polarization,[9] which the first scatter-plot in Figure 3.3 has already shown. The interesting finding here is that the mean level of party system polarization decreases from 4.36, in those cases with a minor centre, to 4.12 in those cases with a medium centre. However, in those cases where the centre is major, the mean level of systemic polarization increases to 4.50 and surpasses the first category. If a trend from these cross-national data is inferred, it is that as long as the centre does not become a major party, its growth is associated with declining levels of polarization. However, when it does

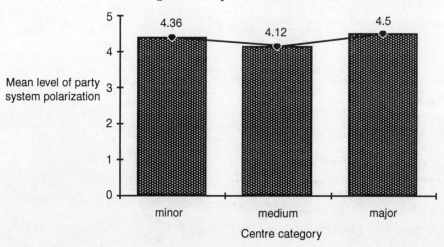

Figure 5.2 Mean polarization level by size of centre parties

become a major party it also becomes associated with a rising level of party system polarization.

The theoretical search for an explanation of the rather stable level of systemic polarization as we move from left to right across the cases on the scatterplot in Figure 3.3, despite the centre parties' increase of parliamentary seats, resulted in the conclusion that this was due to a continuous decline of moderate party parliamentary seats coupled with a rise of extreme party seats. Before delving deeper into the latter relationship between centre and extreme parties, the linear decline of the moderate parties will be addressed.

We now move on to check that the second assumption is empirically valid. The first assumption, upon which this research is based, is that the centre parties are growing. The second assumption – which was supported by the regression analysis – is that in order to maintain a reasonably consistent level of polarization, despite the centre parties' growth, the moderate parties have to show a decrease in their parliamentary strength. By using the same three centre categories, we can see in Figure 5.3 the mean size of the moderate parties as we move from those cases with minor centre parties to those with medium and then major ones.

The second assumption is still valid. As we move from the minor to the medium and finally to the major centre category there is a constant decrease in the size of the moderate parties. Moreover, this pattern appears to be linear, supporting the significant regression results. Is this linear negative relationship between centre and moderate parties true for both the moderate right and the moderate left?

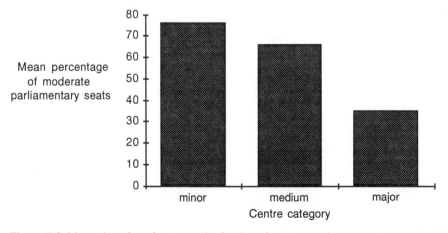

Figure 5.3 Mean size of moderate parties by size of centre parties

When the moderate parties are broken down into the original categories of moderate right and moderate left, both produce negative correlations. At first, however, the size of the moderate right shows a statistically insignificant correlation of $r = -0.306$ in relation to the size of the centre parties.[10] A scatterplot of the results presented in Figure 5.4 provides an explanation: there is a clear negative slope, but three outliers. All three outliers are elections in just one country – Spain. If the Spanish cases are removed, the correlation then becomes significant and rises to $r = -0.761$;[11] if the Spanish cases are not removed, but included as a dummy variable, the correlation also becomes significant and rises to $r = -0.671$.[12]

The moderate left exhibits a strong and significant negative correlation with the centre, and, as Figure 5.5 shows, there appear to be no outliers. The correlation coefficient is $r = -0.711$.[13]

The linear decline of both moderate right and moderate left parties, as we move along the cases where the centre parties increase their share of parliamentary seats, is therefore substantiated by both mean values and regression analysis. The third theoretical assumption can now be tested.

The conclusion that was reached in explaining how the level of polarization was held fairly constant, while the centre parties grew and the moderate parties diminished, was that the extreme parties also had to profit from the decline of the moderate parties. In other words, there could not be a linear decline in the strength of the extreme parties. The regression analysis earlier in this chapter showed that the increase in extreme party seats appears only in those cases where the centre is

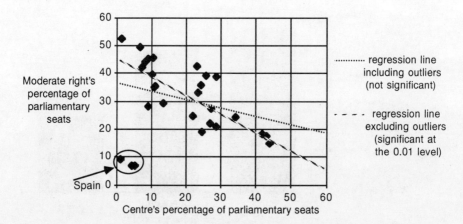

Figure 5.4 Size of moderate right parties with size of centre parties

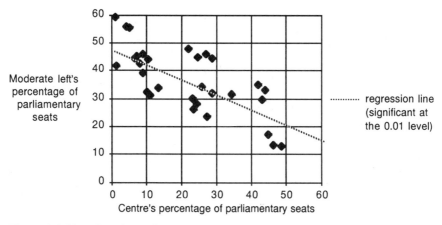

Figure 5.5 Size of moderate left parties with size of centre parties

major – for it is here that polarization rises – rather than in the minor centre category, where the extreme parties decreased their share of seats. Figure 5.6, based on mean values, displays just such a non-linear trend.

This trend corroborates the findings uncovered concerning a 'U'-shaped pattern of extremist growth in Figure 5.1, and also the results found using the mean level of polarization in Figure 5.2. The trend of the extreme parties, much like that of polarization, is not linear.[14] The extreme parties lose strength in those cases where the centre parties initially grow, and the moderate parties decline, producing a lower polarization mean. However, in those cases where the centre parties continue growing, and the moderate parties decline further, the extreme parties bounce back and surpass their previously high mean,

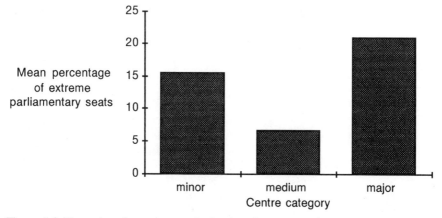

Figure 5.6 Mean size of extreme parties by size of centre parties

producing a higher mean level of polarization than in either of the first two categories. The 'U'-shaped relationship between centre and extreme parties' growth – which produces the non-linear polarization pattern – and the conclusion concerning gains made by the extreme parties at the expense of the moderate parties – when the centre parties continue to expand their parliamentary representation – are corroborated and therefore valid.

In order to show that the extreme parties are growing not just absolutely (i.e. in size) but relatively as well, in the large centre category, the percentage of non-centre parliamentary seats won by either the extreme or the moderate parties can be calculated. The formulas are very simple:

$$\text{Moderate seat percentage of non-centre} = \frac{\text{moderate parties}}{\text{moderate} + \text{extreme parties}}$$

$$\text{Extreme seat percentage of non-centre} = \frac{\text{extreme parties}}{\text{moderate} + \text{extreme parties}}$$

For each of the three centre categories, the two percentages sum to one (Moderate seat percentage of non-centre = 1 − Extreme seat percentage of non-centre, and vice versa). Figure 5.7 shows their relative strengths.

It appears that even in those cases where the moderate parties were declining absolutely, as the centre grew from a minor to a medium-sized party, their relative strength *vis-à-vis* the extreme parties increased from 83 per cent to 91 per cent of the non-centre seats, due to an even

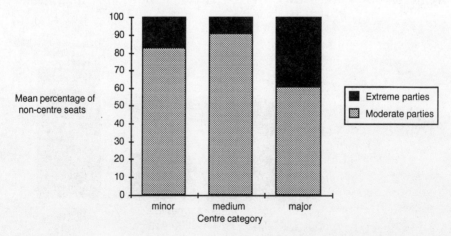

Figure 5.7 Relative size of non-centre moderate and non-centre extreme parties

Table 5.3 Direction of trends

Movement from centre category	Moderate parties		Extreme parties	
	Absolute	Relative	Absolute	Relative
Minor to medium	Decrease	Increase	Decrease	Decrease
Medium to major	Decrease	Decrease	Increase	Increase

more precipitous decline of the extreme parties. However, when we move on to those cases with a major centre, the moderate parties' absolute decline becomes relative as well, from 91 per cent to 61 per cent, while the extreme parties expand beyond their primary size both absolutely and relatively. This further substantiates the non-linear nature of the relationship.[15] A summary of the trends exhibited by both the moderate parties and the extreme parties, in both absolute and relative terms, as we move from the minor to the medium and then to the major centre parties' category, is presented in Table 5.3.

There is, however, one thing which would appear to be a problem that should not be overlooked, although it does not change the general trend of the findings. If a scatterplot of the percentage of non-centre extreme seats is plotted against the size of the centre seats, as presented in Figure 5.8, there appear to be three distinctive outliers.

The three cases in the upper right-hand corner of the plot represent the three Italian elections during the time-frame of this study (these three Italian elections also represented the upper right-hand corner of the plot in Figure 5.1). Could the inordinately high extreme parties' score of the Italian party system be the driving force behind all the previously uncovered non-linear relationships? A quick check shows the answer to be negative.

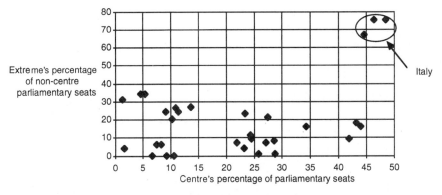

Figure 5.8 Non-centre extreme parties with centre parties

If Italy is removed from the calculation of means, the results obtained do not change the non-linear trend. Despite Italy's exclusion, the third (major) centre category still represents both a higher mean level of party system polarization and a higher mean percentage of extreme parties' seats than the second (medium) category. In the case of polarization means, when Italy is removed the mean level of polarization for the major centre parties category is actually *higher* than when Italy was included.[16] This means that although Italy has an outlying position on the scatterplot, it is not solely responsible for the basic non-linear relationship between the parliamentary strength of extreme parties and centre parties, but only enhances it.

The clearest pattern, based on the differences in means across the three centre categories, is evident if the original outliers uncovered by the first scatterplot are excluded, but Italy is included. Table 5.4 summarizes these mean scores. It must be reiterated that the non-linear relationship does not disappear if the original outliers are included, if Italy is excluded, or both.

According to the table, if we again attempt to elicit a trend from the cross-national data, it is apparent that what keeps the systemic polarization score relatively stable, while the centre parties grow ten-fold, is the presence of non-linear relationships. Polarization actually decreases at first, only to rise again and achieve new heights. The first part of this non-linear trend is propelled by the growth of the centre parties simultaneously with the initial absolute decline of both moderate and extreme parties – further advanced by the moderate parties' relative growth over the extreme parties at this stage. But, as the centre becomes a major party, or group of parties, the second part of the non-linear trend begins when the moderate parties' continued decline becomes not just absolute but also relative, while the extreme parties begin to grow both absolutely and relatively. The steady increase in the strength of the centre parties is offset, in the second stage, by the growth of the extreme parties, which produces not just a relatively constant polarization level, but a slightly increased one.

Table 5.4 Summary of breakdowns by means

Centre category	Level of polarization	Percentage moderates	Percentage extremes	Extreme and moderate seat percentage of non-centre	
Minor	4.36	76.19	15.44	83.14	16.86
Medium	4.12	65.67	6.65	90.71	9.29
Major	4.50	35.00	20.97	60.64	39.36

In summary, although there is a clear negative linear relationship between moderate and centre parties, and between moderate and extreme parties, this does not translate into a positive linear relationship between centre and extreme parties. The relationship here is non-linear – it begins negatively and ends positively – depending on the parliamentary strength of the centre parties. This pattern is what keeps the level of polarization relatively stable. It is not a linear pattern because: (1) the level of party system polarization, when broken down by categories of the centre parties, declines at first and then rises; and (2) the relationship between centre and extreme parties is that of a 'U'-shaped curve. In other words, the extreme parties appear to diminish when we move from those cases with a minor centre to those with a medium one, but increase dramatically when we continue moving to those cases with a major centre. This non-linear pattern is presented visually in Figure 5.9.

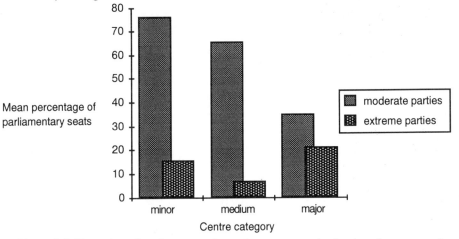

Figure 5.9 Mean size of moderate parties and extreme parties by size of centre parties.

Statistical analysis of European multiparty systems, with proportional representation electoral systems, between 1979 and 1989 leads to the following conclusions:

1. (a) As we move from the cases where the centre is minor to those where it is medium-sized, it gains seats from the moderate parties.
    (b) Simultaneously, the moderate parties gain seats from the extreme parties, thereby diminishing their loss to the centre.
    (c) The overall result is a decline in the level of party system polarization.

2. (a) As we move from the cases where the centre is medium-sized to those where it is major, it still gains seats from the moderate parties.
    (b) Simultaneously, the moderate parties now lose seats to the extreme parties, thereby augmenting their loss to the centre.
    (c) The overall result is a reversal of the previous trend – a stabilization or increase in the level of party system polarization.

5.3   Dichotomous Analysis

The dichotomous categorization of centre parties can now be used to check for linear relationships. When regression analysis is carried out between centre and extreme parties, for only those countries with a small centre, the results are not significant.[17] Linearity, therefore, cannot be assumed for the first set of conclusions elaborated above. When the same regression is run for those countries with a large centre, the results are strongly positive and significant: $r = 0.673$.[18] This outcome substantiates the findings of this study – in those cases where a medium-sized centre continues growing, so do the extreme parties, and thereby polarization is stabilized. The correlations uncovered thus far between centre, moderate and extreme parties are presented in Figure 5.10.

The findings indicate that it is exactly in those cases where the centre is no longer small that the direction of competition changes. In those cases where the centre is small, both moderate and extreme parties lose parliamentary seats – moderate parties lose seats to the centre parties and extreme parties lose seats to the moderate parties – while the level of systemic polarization declines. In other words, the prevalent direction of competition is towards the political centre, i.e. centripetal. Yet in those cases where the centre is large, the moderate parties continue their decline but the extreme parties reverse their earlier loss and win more seats than ever before. The moderate parties now lose seats to both centre and extreme parties – but at a higher ratio to the centre parties – while the level of polarization either remains constant or escalates. The direction of competition is now no longer strictly centripetal. The party system, at this phase, begins showing increasing competition towards the extremes, i.e. centrifugal drives, alongside the centripetal ones. The initial growth of the centre parties and decline of the extreme parties – which exhibits the centripetal trend of the party system in those cases where the centre is small – is shown in Figure 5.11,

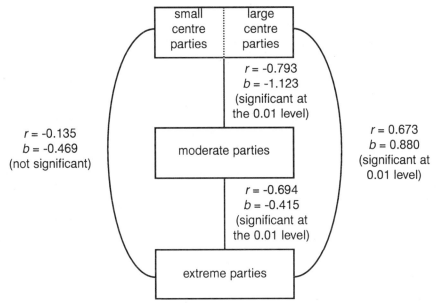

Figure 5.10 Correlations between centre, moderate and extreme parties

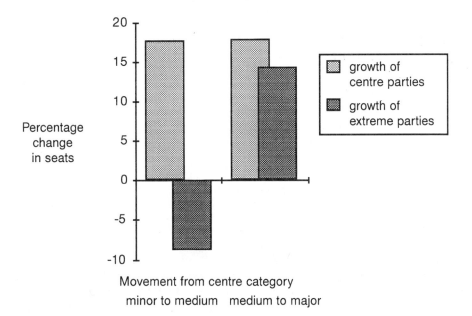

Figure 5.11 Mean change in size of centre and extreme parties

as is the subsequent continued rise of the centre alongside the extreme parties – thereby exhibiting both centripetal and centrifugal competitive patterns in those cases where the centre is large.

Notes

1. $R^2 = 0.629$; $b = -1.123$; significant at the 0.01 level. This excludes the original outliers from the scatterplot. When they are included, the relationship remains: $r = -0.756$; $R^2 = 0.571$; $b = -0.969$; significant at the 0.01 level.

2. $R^2 = 0.481$; $b = -0.415$; significant at the 0.01 level. This also excludes the original outliers. When they are included, the relationship is sustained here as well: $r = -0.610$; $R^2 = 0.372$; $b = -0.387$; significant at the 0.01 level.

3. For the centre, $b = -1.013$; significant at the 0.01 level. For the extremes, $b = -1.018$; significant at the 0.01 level. For the entire multiple regression, $R^2 = 0.991$. These results are obtained when the original outliers are excluded. When the outliers are included, the results are: for the centre, $R = -0.788$, $b = -1.010$; significant at the 0.01 level; for the extremes, $R = -0.649$, $b = -1.021$; significant at the 0.01 level. For the entire multiple regression, $R^2 = 0.991$.

4. For the moderates, $b = -0.965$; significant at the 0.01 level. For the extremes, $b = -0.975$; significant at the 0.01 level. For the entire multiple regression, $R^2 = 0.983$, when the original outliers are excluded. When the outliers are included, the results are: for the moderates, $R = -1.251$, $b = -0.976$; significant at the 0.01 level. For the extremes, $R = -0.812$, $b - -0.997$; significant at the 0.01 level. For the entire multiple regression, $R^2 = 0.985$.

5. $R^2 = 0.015$; $b = 0.103$; significant $t = 0.515$, when the outliers are excluded. When they are included, the already weak relationship is weakened even further: $r = -0.049$; $R^2 = 0.002$; $b = -0.040$, significant $t = 0.778$.

6. The equation is: extreme parties $= ß_0 + ß_1(C - 20\%)^2$, where C is the percentage of centre party seats. A base of 20 per cent was estimated due to the parabola's axis of symmetry produced by this equation, and to the clustering of results in the two scatterplots exhibited in Figures 3.3 and 5.1.

7. $R^2 = 0.268$; $b = 0.028$; significant at the 0.01 level. These results are computed without the original outliers. If they are included, the relationship is: $r = 0.320$; $R^2 = 0.103$; significant only at the 0.06 level. However, in the latter regression, since there are only 31 cases this slight spillover above the universally accepted threshold of 0.05 significance is still acceptable.

8. The outliers uncovered by the first scatterplot (Figure 3.3) are not included in this chart or any of the following charts. Their inclusion, however, would not change the overall non-linear trend for any of the arguments presented herein.

9. The deviation from linearity can be tapped by assessing the difference between r and eta: r is based on a linear regression, while eta does not assume linearity. If eta is larger, and the difference between r and eta is significant, then we can conclude that, despite the groups being homogeneous, they are not related in a linear way. In this case, $r = 0.049$, and eta $= 0.259$, supporting the conclusion that the association is not linear. Moreover, if the mean residual squared is broken down according to the above three centre categories, the results support the presence

of a non-linear association: $\bar{y}_1 = 0.999$; $\bar{y}_2 = 0.110$; $\bar{y}_3 = 1.175$; $r = 0.019$; eta = 0.318.

10. $R^2 = 0.094$; $b = -0.314$; significant $t = 0.113$.

11. $R^2 = 0.579$; $b = -0.667$; significant at the 0.01 level.

12. For the centre: $b = -0.688$; significant at the 0.01 level. For the dummy variable (Spain): $r = -0.710$; $b = -25.930$; significant at the 0.01 level. For the entire equation: $R^2 = 0.465$.

13. $R^2 = 0.506$; $b = -0.560$; significant at the 0.01 level.

14. The deviation from linearity is supported by the difference between the r (0.092) and eta (0.443) scores here as well.

15. $r = -0.357$, while eta = 0.558.

16. 4.55 with Italy excluded, as opposed to 4.50 when Italy was included.

17. $r = -0.136$; $R^2 = 0.019$; $b = -0.469$; significant $t = 0.642$.

18. $R^2 = 0.453$; $b = 0.880$; significant at the 0.01 level.

6

Examining Shifts in Party Positions

6.1 Substantiating Centrifugal Competition

In order to accept the second hypothesized explanation of the relationship between the centre and polarization, as previously elaborated in
Chapter 4, it must be shown that as we move from cases with a minor
centre to those with medium-sized and major centres, either moderate
or extreme parties, or both, move away from the centre along the left–
right scale.

In Chapter 5 it was established that a three-fold categorization of
countries, according to the parliamentary size of the centre parties,
uncovered non-linear trends in both the level of party system polarization and the parliamentary strength of extreme parties. A dichotomous
categorization showed that these trends correspond with radically
different correlations between centre and extreme parties. In adopting
either division, into three or just two categories, a mean location along
the left–right scale of each party category needs to be determined, in
order to see if either moderate or extreme parties move away from the
centre. Producing this measure is a two-step process.

First, a weighted locational score must be elaborated for each of the
five categories that make up the 10-point, left–right scale. This is
achieved by multiplying the location of each party along this scale by its
share of the parliamentary seats for the category it belongs to, and
summing the results for each election. A *weighted mean* is thus calculated
for each separate category. For example, let us assume that two parties
from the moderate right category won parliamentary seats in an election; one has 10 per cent of the parliamentary seats and the other has 20
per cent. The left–right location of the first party is multiplied by one-

third – the proportion of seats that this party holds in its category – and the left–right location of the second party is multiplied by two-thirds. A summation of these two results produces a weighted mean for the moderate right for that particular election.

Second, a weighted mean score for each of the five categories is averaged over time across all the cases within a particular category of the centre – minor, medium and major for the three-fold categorization; small and large for the dichotomous one. Do the findings support the second explanation which posited that parties were moving in a centrifugal pattern along the left–right scale?

Figure 6.1 shows the weighted mean for each of the five categories when the three-fold categorization is adopted. It is immediately apparent that both moderate categories exhibit a linear decline in their share of seats coupled with a centrifugal pattern of movement within their range along the left–right scale. The two extreme categories, on the other hand, present opposing and reversed patterns concerning both their share of seats and their movement on the left–right scale.

The moderate right category decreases its share of seats from 33 per cent in those cases with a minor centre, to 30 per cent in the medium centre cases, and finally to 11 per cent as we reach the major centre category. Its movement on the left-right continuum is from 7.0 to 7.3 and then to 7.4, respectively. The moderate left category exhibits an almost identical pattern, decreasing its share of seats from 43 per cent to 35 per cent and finally to 24 per cent, as we move from minor to

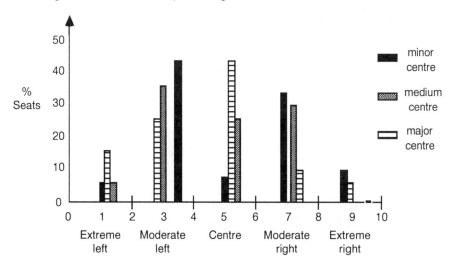

Figure 6.1 Mean category location and seat percentage by minor, medium and major centre

medium and then to major centre cases, while moving centrifugally from 3.5 to 2.9 and then to 2.8.

Both moderate categories are losing a similar share of seats, but the moderate left parties move almost twice the distance of the moderate right parties. The more intense centrifugal movement of the moderate left parties is magnified by their bigger share of the parliamentary seats over the moderate right parties, in all three centre categories. Example 7 (Table 4.7) has already shown that a centrifugal movement of parties can overcome a centripetal movement of voters, and result in an increase of party system polarization. The centrifugal movement of the two moderate categories, and the stronger shift exhibited by the larger moderate left category, would lead to the conclusion that their impact on polarization is both positive and constant.

The two extreme categories do not show any clear pattern. Both decrease their share of seats at first, and then increase it. However, the extreme right parties possess 10 per cent of the seats in those cases with a minor centre, which declines dramatically to less than 1 per cent in the medium centre category and rises to 5 per cent in the large centre category. They therefore end up with less than one-half of the seats that they started with. The extreme left, on the other hand, shows an increase of seats from 6 per cent in the first two categories to 16 per cent in the third centre category. They, in total contradiction to the extreme right parties, end up with over twice as many seats as they began with.

The movement of the two extreme categories along the left–right scale is contradictory as well. The weighted mean of the extreme right is found at 8.7 in those cases with a minor centre, then it is located as far out as 9.6 in the medium centre cases, and it moves back in to 9.2 when the centre is major. When it moves sharply outwards it loses almost all of its seats, thereby diminishing the positive impact it could have had on the level of polarization. Then, as it moves partially inwards again, it gains seats and has a significantly negative impact on systemic polarization. It thus appears that the only impact the extreme right parties have on the level of polarization is a negative one, in those cases with a major centre.

The weighted mean of the extreme left is at 1.2 in those cases with a minor centre, and then it moves inwards to 1.5 for the medium centre category, and back out to 1.3 when the centre is major. The first, and stronger, centripetal move is not magnified because the extreme left's share of seats remains constant, whereas the subsequent and smaller centrifugal move is strongly amplified by almost a tripling of its share of seats. The extreme left would appear to contribute slightly negatively to the level of polarization at first, but then both reverses and increases its impact to become significant and positive.

The negligible, or slightly negative, impact on systemic polarization which the extreme parties have – when we move between those cases where the centre is minor to those where it is of medium size – leads to the conclusion that the positive impact on the level of polarization is due to the centrifugal pattern exhibited largely by the moderate parties. The positive impact of the extreme left on systemic polarization – when we move from those cases where the centre is medium to those where it is major – is the opposite of the negative impact that the extreme right has on polarization. The two extreme categories appear to offset each other in this second comparison of cases, leaving it, once again, up to the centrifugal trend of the moderate parties to impact positively on the level of party system polarization.

By allowing the categories to vary not only in parliamentary size but also in their positions on the left–right scale, it is possible to assess their overall impact on the level of party system polarization. Example 9, in Table 6.1, uses the means from each centre category in Figure 6.1 as separate election results, producing a non-linear pattern of systemic polarization which supports the case for the second hypothesis. The level of party system polarization does indeed decline from 4.5, in those cases with a minor centre, to 4.0 in the medium centre category, only to achieve a new high for those cases with a major centre, 4.7. This result is congruent with Figure 5.2, based on the three-fold categorization, which showed that the mean level of polarization declined at first but then rose to reach a new high.

The three-fold categorization thus supports the argument made in the second hypothetical explanation, which concentrates on party movement as the variable which counters the polarization measure's

Table 6.1 Example 9

Election	1		2		3	
	L-R	%	L-R	%	L-R	%
Centre parties	5.1	8	5.6	26	5.4	43
Moderate right parties	7.0	33	7.3	30	7.4	11
Moderate left parties	3.5	43	2.9	35	2.8	24
Extreme right parties	8.7	10	9.6	0	9.2	5
Extreme left parties	1.2	6	1.5	6	1.3	16
Polarization	4.5		4.0		4.7	

proclivity to decline when centre parties increase their share of parliamentary seats. Would this argument hold up if the dichotomous categorization was adopted? Would we still see an increase in systemic polarization when we moved between the two categories of small and large centre parties?

The dichotomous findings do indeed corroborate the assumptions of the second explanation. The weighted mean of three out of four categories surrounding the centre – moderate right, moderate left and extreme right – are found further from the middle as we move from those cases with a small centre to those with a large centre. Only the extreme left opposed this trend, and was found to move slightly inwards. The two locations for each of the five categories, in accordance with their parliamentary sizes for each location, are shown in Figure 6.2.

The dark bars are closer to the centre than the shaded bars for all but the extreme left category. The moderate right declines from an average of 33 per cent of the parliamentary seats in those countries where the centre is small, to 22 per cent of the seats in the countries with a large centre. During this decline it moves outwards from a mean location of 7.0 to 7.4 within its range. The moderate left likewise declines from 43 per cent to 31 per cent of the seats, and also moves outwards from 3.5 to 2.8.

The extreme right declines from 10 per cent of the seats in countries with a small centre to 2 per cent in those where the centre is large. It

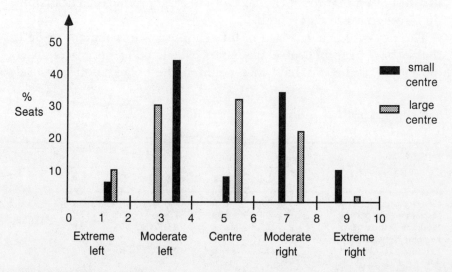

Figure 6.2 Mean category location and seat percentage by small and large centre

moves outwardly from 8.7 to 9.3 on the continuum while it declines. The extreme left, however, increases from 6 per cent to 10 per cent of the seats and moves in from 1.2 to 1.4. It is interesting to note that only the extreme left category showed a moderating trend and is also the only one to show growth alongside the centre parties.

The offsetting patterns exhibited by the two extremes seem to lessen their effect. Most of the impact on reversing the proclivity of the polarization measure to decline as the centre grows appears, yet again, to belong to the centrifugal pattern of both moderate right and moderate left parties. Both move approximately one-half of a point along the 10-point scale, which is a significant 25 per cent of their total range.

If we take the figures reported above and measure the level of party system polarization, allowing the categories to vary in both size and location, will the level of polarization remain relatively constant? Example 10, in Table 6.2, presents the answer. The first election uses the weighted mean scores from Figure 6.2 where the centre is small, and the second election uses the weighted results for countries where the centre is large. The result is exactly what the scatterplot of cases in Figure 3.3 produced. The level of polarization has remained constant, despite the more than four-fold growth of the centre.

6.2 Blaming the Moderate Parties

The mean locations of the party categories along the left–right scale can also be regressed with the parliamentary size of the centre parties, thereby providing an additional test for the second hypothesis. The results lend further support to the finding reached thus far: the moderate right and left parties both move in a centrifugal pattern, but the trends of the extreme right and left parties appear to offset each other.

Table 6.2 Example 10

Election	1		2	
	L-R	%	L-R	%
Centre parties	5.1	8	5.5	33
Moderate right parties	7.0	33	7.4	22
Moderate left parties	3.5	43	2.8	31
Extreme right parties	8.7	10	9.3	2
Extreme left parties	1.2	6	1.4	10
Polarization		4.5		4.5

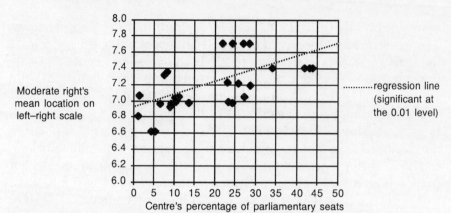

Figure 6.3 Size of centre parties with weighted moderate right

With the use of regression analysis, once again the moderate categories show significant relationships between the size of the centre parties and their mean location on the left–right scale. The mean location of the moderate right has a significant positive relationship with the parliamentary size of the centre of $r = 0.621$.[1] That is, as Figure 6.3 shows, in those cases where the centre is large, the mean location of the moderate right category moves further to the right in a centrifugal pattern.

The mean location of the moderate left has a significant negative relationship with the size of the centre of $r = -0.716$.[2] This means that in those cases where the centre is large, the mean location of the moderate left category is located further to the left, thereby also exhibiting a centrifugal trend as presented in Figure 6.4.

When the mean location of the extreme right is correlated with the centre a significant positive relationship is produced.[3] However, as

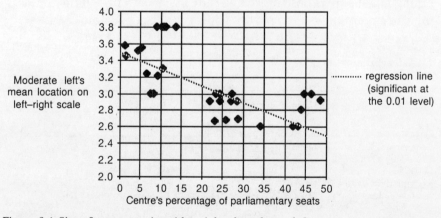

Figure 6.4 Size of centre parties with weighted moderate left

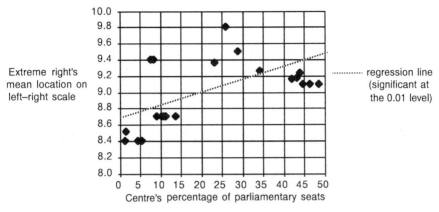

Figure 6.5 Size of centre parties with weighted extreme right

Figure 6.5 shows, this result is based on heteroskedastic data and thus infringes on one of the assumptions necessary for inferring any relationship based on statistical correlations.

If the centre is once again dichotomized, an insignificant result is obtained when regressing the mean location of the extreme right with the small centre category,[4] and a significant negative result is obtained when regressing between the mean location of the extreme right and the large centre category.[5] There seems to be no relationship between a small centre and the mean location of the extreme right – the latter fluctuates randomly within its range on the left–right scale and does not influence the level of party system polarization. There is, however, a linear relationship between a large centre and the mean location of the extreme right – the latter moves centripetally in those cases where the centre is large, thereby lowering the level of polarization. The extreme

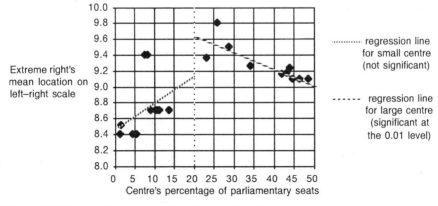

Figure 6.6 Weighted extreme right with small and large centre

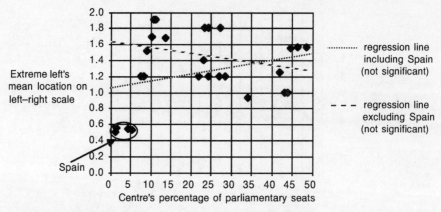

Figure 6.7 Size of centre parties with weighted extreme left

right, therefore, has only a negative impact on polarization and then only when the centre is large. These results are presented in Figure 6.6.

The relationship between the parliamentary size of the centre parties and the mean location of the extreme left parties is insignificant.[6] But, as Figure 6.7 shows, it appears as though there are outliers that might be impacting the regression coefficient, all of which represent elections in Spain. When Spain is removed, the regression changes direction but still remains insignificant.[7]

Dichotomizing the centre in the attempt to discern any underlying trends yields significant results only for the small centre category. In those cases where the centre is small, there is a strongly positive relationship between it and the mean location of the extreme left,

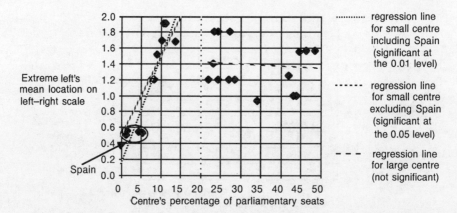

Figure 6.8 Weighted extreme left with small and large centre

whether Spain is included or excluded.[8] The extreme left moves centripetally as we move from left to right across the small centre cases, reducing the level of party system polarization. In those cases with a large centre, the relationship becomes insignificant,[9] and the extreme left fluctuates randomly within its range on the left–right scale and does not influence the level of polarization. The extreme left, therefore, has only a negative impact on polarization and then only in the small centre cases. These results are presented in Figure 6.8.

In summary, the extreme parties appear to have only a moderating impact on polarization. As we move from left to right in the scatterplots across the small centre cases, the extreme left moves centripetally and the extreme right moves randomly. As we continue moving from left to right across the large centre cases, the extreme right moves centripetally and the extreme left moves randomly. Overall, when the extreme parties are merged, there is a constant centripetal pattern exhibited, but never a centrifugal one.

The measures utilized thus far provide the following conclusions, as we move across the various scatterplots from left to right: (1) both moderate right and left categories move in a centrifugal pattern, thereby impacting positively on the level of party system polarization; (2) both extreme right and left categories either move randomly or centripetally, thereby impacting negatively on systemic polarization. *The centrifugal movement of the moderate parties must, therefore, be the driving force behind the relatively consistent level of polarization, despite their loss of seats to the centre parties.* This finding is somewhat similar to those uncovered from Figure 6.2 and Example 10 (Table 6.2). Furthermore, Example 7 (Table 4.7) has already shown that even a decline in the size of the moderate parties, coupled by a movement away from the centre, results in an increase in the level of polarization.

This conclusion is strengthened and refined when the findings of the first theoretical explanation – now backed by empirical evidence – are incorporated. The first explanation posited that the parliamentary strength of the centre parties is positively associated with that of the extreme parties, but only in those cases where the centre is large. The evidence in this chapter argues that only one category of the extreme parties moves centripetally when the centre is either small or large. A synthesis of these two produces the conclusion that the influence of the extreme parties' location on the left–right scale on the level of polarization is stronger when the centre is large. That is, in the cases where the centre is small, the impact of the centripetal trend exhibited by the extreme left is not enhanced, because the parliamentary strength of the extremes is fluctuating randomly. However, in the cases where the centre is large, the influence of the centripetal trend manifested by the extreme right is magnified by the simultaneous rise in its share of parliamentary seats.

Therefore, since it is the centrifugal movement of the moderate parties that is countering the extreme parties' centripetal and moderating influence, in order to keep the level of polarization constant the centrifugal trend of the moderate parties must be stronger when the centre is large than when it is small. That is, in order to combat the growing parliamentary strength of the centre parties and the centripetal movement of the extreme parties – in those cases where the centre is large – the declining moderate parties must enhance their centrifugal movement. The validity of these explanations will be tested, in an intense manner, in the next part.

Notes

1. $R^2 = 0.386$; $b = 0.015$; significant at the 0.01 level.
2. $R^2 = 0.513$; b $= -0.020$; significant at the 0.01 level.
3. $r = 0.558$; $R^2 = 0.312$; $b = 0.013$; significant at the 0.01 level.
4. $r = 0.356$; $R^2 = 0.127$; $b = 0.032$; significant $t = 0.283$.
5. $r = -0.825$; $R^2 = 0.681$; $b = -0.020$; significant at the 0.01 level.
6. $r = 0.248$; $R^2 = 0.062$; $b = 0.007$; significant $t = 0.222$.
7. $r = -0.318$; $R^2 = 0.101$; $b = -0.007$; significant $t = 0.149$.
8. When Spain is included: $r = 0.922$; $R^2 = 0.850$; $b = 0.133$; significant at the 0.01 level. When Spain is excluded: $r = 0.745$; $R^2 = 0.554$; $b = 0.106$; significant at the 0.05 level.
9. $r = -0.166$; $R^2 = 0.028$; $b = 0.005$; significant $t = 0.555$.

Part III

Empirical Inquiry

7

Two Cases: Denmark and The Netherlands, 1945–90

7.1 The Cases

The previous chapters argued that strong centre parties may lead to polarization, not moderation. This study showed that as the centre's share of parliamentary seats increased, this convergence of voters was offset by two concurrent and divergent party trends. As the centre parties expanded, either: (1) the extreme parties increased as well; or (2) an outward movement of moderate parties took place. This part sets out to test these two trends in order to assess which is more valid according to two case studies, since each pattern has a different impact on electoral competition and governmental stability. The results show that the centre is indeed related to systemic polarization, but that one of the two patterns is invalid.

The case studies chosen seek to indicate exactly how the centre influences the two diametrically diverging patterns of party competition. However, there is no clear-cut choice of countries available to achieve this goal, for several reasons. First, both the trichotomous and dichotomous categorizations of the centre produce a list of mutually exclusive countries. There is no one country in which the centre can be analysed as it grows from being a minor to a medium and finally to a major-sized party, or from even one category to the next. This means that the entire analysis is based on a cross-sectional comparison, and not country-specific growth over time. Second, apart from the medium-sized centre category, in which all three countries are clustered together on the polarization index, the other two centre categories produce countries with large differences in either intra-country or inter-country polarization scores. For example, inter-country differences can be illustrated by the fact that the lowest mean polarization score is that of Germany (3.28), found in the minor centre category, while the highest mean polarization score is that of Norway (5.87), also from the minor centre category. Intra-country differences are exhibited by Norway, which has polarization scores ranging from 5.10 to 7.34, a larger variation than that of the 31 cases in the horizontal clustering between 3.14 and 5.23 in the original scatterplot of the centre and polarization (Figure 3.3).

This could mean that we are confronted with only cross-sectional patterns, which might not be sustained within any of the countries included in the cross-national data. Moreover, due to the mutual exclusivity of the centre categories, the patterns uncovered could be the result of idiosyncratic country variables that lack any generalizable referents. That is, the statistical findings in the previous chapters could have been produced by inferring a relationship across countries that may not really be there. However, it is hard to believe that the associations identified, and the propositions elaborated, are all based on a spurious statistical association. The findings uncovered are not simple statistical assertions; they are probabilistic propositions based both theoretically and empirically on identification and explanation. Thus, in order to substantiate these findings, the dynamic components of the hypothesized relationship need to be pursued through case studies.

The proposed relationship will be analysed in depth by following the line of logic revealed by the regression analysis. The regression analysis adopted the dichotomous categorization of countries in the search for linear relationships – countries with either a small or a large centre – and produced radically different results for each category. One country will be chosen from each centre category. Each country should have a similar level of systemic polarization, conforming with the horizontal clustering of cases in the original centre and polarization scatterplot.

The adoption of this strategy points to several possible case studies: Denmark, Germany, Norway or Spain for the small centre category; Belgium, Finland, Sweden, Austria, Italy or The Netherlands for the large centre category. Denmark was chosen to represent those countries with a small centre due to drawbacks in the other countries. Norway exhibits extremely high volatility in its systemic polarization scores, and had one election that belonged in the group of outliers, which have been excluded from this study thus far. Spain belongs to the group of party systems that have emerged from a transition to democracy from authoritarianism. The early years of such a newly formed democratic party system could produce rather turbulent voter volatility impacting both on centre parties and party system polarization, but being a poor indicator of any relationship between the two.[1] Germany has the lowest mean polarization score, and would thus appear as a choice for a simple confirmation of the findings concerning the small centre category.

The Netherlands was chosen to represent those cases in the large centre category. Belgium was eliminated because of its unique segmented society. Austria was ruled out because all three of its elections belong to the group of outliers which this study has excluded. Italy was not chosen for similar reasons used to reject Germany – its inclusion would serve as the most obvious hypothesis confirming choice. This leaves Finland, Sweden and The Netherlands. Finland has always been considered a unique case, due to the impact of its proximity to the former Soviet Union. Sweden would have provided a second Scandinavian case study. The choice of The Netherlands is simply because it does not provide a clear reason for preclusion, and is quite similar to Denmark in many aspects – particularly polarization, as shown in Table 7.1 – which allow for variables exogenous to the party system to be controlled.

This chapter presents a cursory description of the party systems of the two countries, along with their development in the post-war period. Chapter 8 assesses the applicability of the unidimensional left–right socio-economic scale – on which the model is based – for both countries, and analyses in a more intense manner the categorization of parties into the centre and the extremes. Chapters 9 and 10 are devoted to an investigation of the two explanations concerning the centre's relationship with polarization – movement of voter support and shifts in party positions – in each of the two case studies.

7.2 The Danish Party System

Following World War II, a new constitution was drawn up and, after being approved in a referendum, came into force in 1953. The constitution abolished the second chamber and made the Danish parliament

Table 7.1 The case studies

Country	Centre	Mean level of party system polarization
Denmark	Small	4.37
The Netherlands	Large	4.55

unicameral, consisting of only the Folketing. This popularly elected chamber has 179 members, of which four are elected in Greenland and the Faroe Islands,[2] while the remaining 175 are elected in Denmark proper. The seats are distributed according to a complicated form of proportional representation.[3]

Comparative typologies generated in the 1950s and 1960s classified the stable Danish political system as a working multiparty system (Rustow, 1956), the political culture as homogeneous and secularized (Almond and Verba, 1963), and the party system as frozen in the 1920s (Lipset and Rokkan, 1967). Yet by 1970, Dahl (1970: 4) noticed that 'some of the most profound changes in the world take place in a quiet country like Denmark'. Three years later, Denmark experienced an election that elicited observers to come up with new phrases to encapsulate the extent of the unprecedented and massive change which had taken place. In the aftermath of the 1973 election, scholars concluded that the Danes had administered an 'electoral shock to their party system', a 'landslide protest election', an 'electoral earthquake', a 'cataclysmic change'. Rusk and Borre (1974: 330) wrote that 'if Denmark was ever to become a laboratory setting for studying political change, the time seems clearly at hand'.

The fundamental characteristic of Danish politics, both before and still to some extent after 1973, has been called consensual (Elder *et al.*, 1982), coalescent (Pedersen, 1987), or basically co-operative parliamentarism (Fitzmaurice, 1981). Such a pattern of decision-making is produced by pragmatic and tolerant parties who are willing to negotiate and bargain.

From the beginning of the twentieth century there have been four major and constant parties in Danish politics – or, as they are usually called, the 'four old parties'. The four core parties are the Social Democrats (SD), the Radical Liberals (RV), the Liberals (V) and the Conservatives (KF). New competitors have come and gone, but these four parties have continued, even after 1973, to occupy the central role in the Danish party system and to dominate in the allocation of parliamentary seats during this century, as Table 7.2 shows.

Table 7.2 Average percentage of four old parties' seats, 1947–90

1947–71 (10 elections)	1973–90 (9 elections)
90%	68%

This pattern of seat distribution has led most students of Danish politics to divide the post-war period into two phases: pre- and post-1973. The former is the old party system in which four major actors dominated over alternating minor contenders; while the latter is a new party system made up of an average of ten parties, some of which are relatively permanent and important competitors to the old parties.

The largest of the old parties was the SD, which obtained an average of 40 per cent of the seats from 1945 to 1971 (Table 7.3). In collaboration with the smallest of the old parties, the RV, the SD managed to stay in control of government for extended periods. The alternative governing coalition consisted of the two medium-sized 'bourgeois' parties, the V and the KF, who held a relatively balanced position *vis-à-vis* the SD.

The relative parity between the RV and the KF on the one hand, and the SD on the other, can be better perceived if the party system is divided into the five categories making up the left–right scale depicted in Figure 7.1. The relative weakness of the Danish centre also becomes apparent in this figure, and it was at times equivalent in strength to the extreme left. A third interesting factor is that there is no extreme right category which achieved parliamentary representation in the old Danish party system.

This numerical balance shaped the formation of governing coalitions, and formed a basis of relatively fixed patterns of co-operation. For almost twenty years, from 1947 to 1968 (except for 1950–53), the SD was the governing party relying on either a formal coalition with the RV or on its parliamentary support. A change of parties within the extreme

Table 7.3 Numerical distribution of Folketing seats, 1945–71

Party	1945	1947	1950	1953[a]	1953[b]	1957	1960	1964	1966	1968	1971
Communist (DKP)	18	9	7	7	8	6					
Socialist People's (SF)							11	10	20	11	17
Social Democratic (SD)	48	57	59	61	74	70	76	76	69	62	70
Radical Liberal (RV)	11	10	12	13	14	14	11	10	13	27	27
Justice (DR)	3	6	12	9	6	9					
Liberal (V)	38	49	32	33	42	45	38	38	35	34	30
Conservative (KF)	26	17	27	26	30	30	32	36	34	37	31
Others		4				1	1	7	5	4	4
Faroes and Greenland	1	1	2	4	4	4	4	4	4	4	4
Total	149	149	151	153	179	179	179	179	179	179	179

[a] April; [b] September; four old parties appear in bold; parties are listed on a scale from left to right; initials in parentheses are the official abbreviations

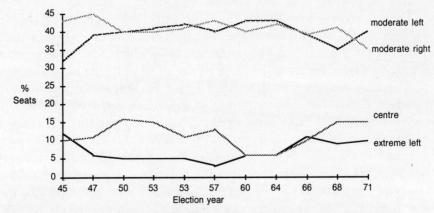

extreme left = Communists (1945–47) + Socialist People's (1960–71) + Left Socialists (1968)
moderate left = Social Democrats (1945–71)
centre = Radical Liberals (1945–71) + Justice (1945–57)
moderate right = Liberals (1945–71) + Conservatives (1945–71)

Figure 7.1 Party blocs' percentages of Folketing seats, 1945–71

left during the 1960s brought this pattern of co-operation to an end. In 1960, the Socialist People's Party (SF) appeared on the parliamentary stage, replacing the Communist Party (DKP), from which it had broken off only two years earlier (see Table 7.3). By 1966, its gains produced a 'workers'' majority in the Folketing for the first time. The SD then ceased to shun its leftist competitor and began to co-operate informally with the SF. This swing to the left on the part of the SD pushed the RV towards the 'bourgeois' bloc, and the three parties formed their first coalition after the 1968 elections. From then on, the RV perceived its role as a balancing one between the two blocs, refusing to become too closely associated with either.

Rustow attributed the persistence of what he calls the Danish four-party system

> primarily to the fact that it closely reflects the social structure ... and that social and economic differences today provide the main stimulus for party division. The Conservative [KF], Agrarians [V] and Socialists [SD] represent the interests of employers, farmers and workers, respectively. Those middle class elements not readily identified with any of these groups have provided the chief support for the Liberal [RV] parties. (Rustow, 1956: 176)

The Scandinavian countries in general have had the highest level of class voting in Europe, higher even than the British two-party system, and of all the Scandinavian countries 'Denmark exhibits the least deviation from the class party pattern', according to Worre (1980: 303).

Figure 7.2 presents a graphic representation of the old Danish party system, clearly exhibiting an overwhelming majority of parliamentary seats concentrated within and around the centre of the left–right scale.

The magnitude of the change brought about by the 1973 election is still reverberating throughout the Danish party system. In measures of aggregate electoral volatility, this election ranks highest of all European post-war elections (Pedersen, 1979). The five parties represented in the Folketing all lost seats. On average, the incumbent parties lost over one-third of their seats, while simultaneously five new parties entered the Folketing and parliamentary fractionalization rose to its highest point ever. It is important to note that more than one-half of those supporters who abandoned the incumbent parties voted for new extremist parties (Table 7.4).

The post-1973 party system can be divided into five groups: extreme left, moderate left, centre (sometimes referred to as the bourgeois or non-socialist centre), moderate right (sometimes labelled the bourgeois right) and extreme right. The parties belonging to each group are presented in Table 7.5.

These categories are utilized to present a clearer picture of the election results, in order to compare them with those of the old party system, as seen in Figure 7.3. Immediately, one notices that the fifth

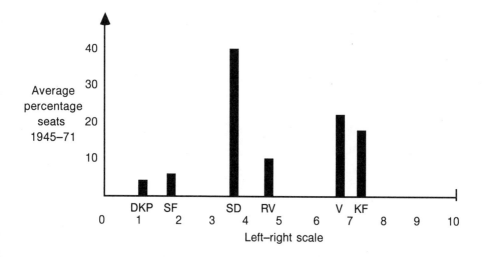

Figure 7.2 The old Danish party system

Table 7.4 Numerical distribution of Folketing seats, 1973–90

Party	1973	1975	1977	1979	1981	1984	1987	1988	1990
Left Socialist (VS)		4	5	6	5	5			
Communist (DKP)	6	7	7						
Socialist People's (SF)	11	9	7	11	21	21	27	24	15
Social Democratic (SD)	46	53	65	68	59	56	54	55	69
Radical Liberal (RV)	20	13	6	10	9	10	11	10	7
Justice (DR)		5		6	5				
Centre Democratic (CD)	14	4	11	6	15	8	9	9	9
Christian People's (KRF)	7	9	6	5	4	5	4	4	4
Liberal (V)	22	42	21	22	20	22	19	22	29
Conservative (KF)	16	10	15	22	26	42	38	35	30
Progress (FRP)	28	24	26	20	16	6	9	16	12
Others								4	
Faroes and Greenland	4	4	4	4	4	4	4	4	4
Total	179	179	179	179	179	179	179	179	179

Parties are listed on a scale from left to right; four old parties appear in bold; initials in parentheses are the official abbreviations

category, the extreme right, which was empty in the old party system (see Figures 7.1 and 7.2), has been filled. The extreme right, once it achieved parliamentary representation and despite the losses during its first decade, has managed to remain in the Folketing and to close in on the centre and extreme left. The gains and losses of the extreme right appear to have come from the moderate right, which suffered a decade of inferiority in comparison to the moderate left, but regained its position of parity. The centre seems to have changed the least, barring the 1973 election, and is generally weaker than the total of the two extremes.

The old party system was swept away in 1973, and in its place the new Danish party system exhibited an extraordinary parliamentary stalemate. The era of consensus was replaced by a situation of 'extreme minority parliamentarism', defined as minority governments lacking permanent majority coalitions who are frequently outvoted by the opposing majority without stepping down (Nielsen and Pedersen,

Table 7.5 Party groups in the new (post-1973) Danish party system

Extreme left	Moderate left	Centre	Moderate right	Extreme right
VS, DKP, SF	SD	RV, DR, CD, KRF	V, KF	FRP

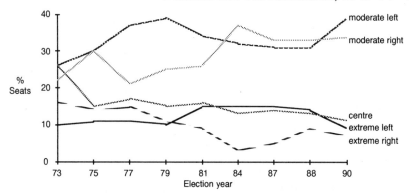

extreme left = Left Socialists (1975–84) + Communists (1973–77) + Socialist People's (1973–90)
moderate left = Social Democrats (1973–90)
centre = Radical Liberals (1973–90) + Justice (1973, 1977–79) + Centre Democrats (1973–90)
    + Christian People's (1973–90)
moderate right = Liberals (1973–90) + Conservatives (1973–90)
extreme right = Progress (1973–90)

Figure 7.3 Party blocs' percentages of Folketing seats, 1973–90

1989). Denmark did not have a majority government in the entire 1973–90 period.

The upheaval of 1973 brought about the rapid decay of the old party system. Part of the stability of the old system resulted from the fact that party support was to a high degree determined by social structure. This linkage began to erode in the 1960s, and could no longer be sustained in the 1970s. The new parties were not linked to social classes in the same way as the old ones were. Moreover, they differed considerably in tactics, perception and ideological inclination from all the old and old/

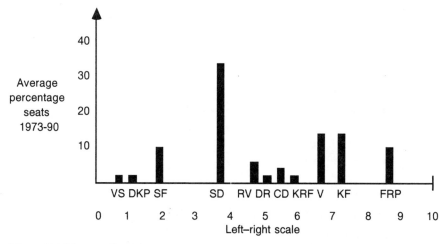

Figure 7.4 The new Danish party system

new parties. Socio-economic change reduced party attachments, which, in turn, increased electoral mobility and undermined the stability of the old party system (Jarlov and Kristensen, 1978).

Figure 7.4 presents a graphic description of the new party system. The fragmentation of the new system in comparison to the old one (Figure 7.2) is apparent, as is the fact that an increasing number of parliamentary seats are now located away from the area in or around the centre of the left–right scale.

7.3   The Dutch Party System

Legislative authority resides in the bicameral Staten Generaal. The upper chamber, the Eerste Kamer, is composed of 75 members indirectly elected by the provincial legislatures for 6-year terms. The lower and more important chamber, the Tweede Kamer, consists of 150 members directly elected by proportional representation for 4-year terms.[4]

The major political parties in the post-war Dutch party system enjoyed rather stable electoral support and a lack of fragmentation. This was largely due to the peculiar characteristic of Dutch politics that each main party had its own stable electoral clientele, or bloc. Almost all Catholics, who number close to 40 per cent of the electorate, supported the Catholic People's Party (KVP) and made it the biggest party routinely gaining one-third of the seats in the Tweede Kamer. The Orthodox Reformed Church backed the Anti-Revolutionary Party (ARP), while the Dutch Reformed Church members voted for the Christian Historical Union (CHU), together usually obtaining over one-fifth of the seats. For half a century, since the introduction of universal suffrage in 1917, the adherence of religious voters to religious parties won them a majority. The non-religious voters were divided between the Labour (PvdA) and Liberal (VVD) parties, the former gaining one-third of the seats and the latter usually winning no more than 10 per cent. Other parties existed, and gained parliamentary representation. An average of a dozen parties have sat in the Tweede Kamer since 1918, but the five major parties dominated in parliament and monopolized government.

The Dutch party system was based on five main and distinct subcultures. 'Parties were therefore largely the visible sentinels of complex social systems,' according to Daalder (1979: 177). The Dutch party system, and Dutch society for that matter, has been described as being based on pillars, or, to use the Dutch term, *zuilen* (Rokkan, 1977).

Large-scale autonomous social organizations encompassed all aspects of Dutch life and performed all social functions from the cradle to the grave – schools, newspapers, trade unions, business and farming associations, sport and social clubs, etc. *Verzuiling*, pillarization based on social segmentation, was the characteristic feature of Dutch society and was reflected in the constellation and strengths of the parties. The five parties which represented the pillars were not only the strongest electorally, but were also the only ones to participate in government, and came to define the party system. For that reason they have become known as the five system parties.

Political conflict between the pillars was defused by the creation of an elaborate system of power-sharing. Advisory bodies, in which each *zuil* was proportionally represented, fashioned careful elite compromises. A tradition of accepting expert advice grew and made this elaborate process both functional and effective. Divisive issues were left to each separate subculture, and autonomy over the decision-making process was granted. This model of Dutch democracy was designated as consociationalism by Lijphart (1968). Its features reinforced the subcultural organizational structures, and political parties assumed the role of defending subcultural interests at the governmental level, while safeguarding subcultural autonomy where government intervention could be avoided.

By the 1960s, fundamental cracks could be discerned in the once impregnable religious subcultures. A massive decline in church attendance was the most visible signal, but others – such as the increase in both social and physical mobility and the rise to prominence of the mass media – had a similar impact. The control exercised by the religious pillars began to crumble, and the organizational structures of their pillars fell into disarray. Some subcultural institutions broke away from their particular *zuil* and formed a new, independent organization which sought to deemphasize religious attachment, others fused with non-religious organizations, while still others simply broke down. The result was that the influence of religious beliefs as a decisive factor in personal, social and political behaviour declined. The combined strength of the three religious parties fell in less than one decade by more than one-third – from 51 per cent in 1963 to 32 per cent in 1972. As the religious parties lost their parliamentary majority, the aggregate strength of the five main system parties declined and new parties began to challenge their hegemony (Table 7.6).

The interaction between parties also changed. Accommodation was replaced by adversarial confrontation, and coalescence by polarization.

Table 7.6 Average percentage of five system parties' seats, 1946–89

1946–63 (6 elections)	1967–89 (8 elections)
91%	82%

This change led Lijphart, in the second edition of his work, to write that

> the system of accommodation reached its heyday in the 1950s but declined rapidly in the following decade. By the late 1960s, it had broken down completely. The Second Chamber elections of 1967 marked the turning point, and this year can therefore be regarded as the end of half a century of accommodation politics. (Lijphart, 1975: 196–7)

In short, 1967 represents a change that is only partially reflected in the Dutch election results. The political parties have successfully recovered somewhat from their decline, but the framework of Dutch politics experienced a considerable and significant change.

The religious parties had a constant majority in parliament between 1946 and 1967, and could thereby determine the composition of all governments – provided they did not quarrel with each other. Under such a condition, the Liberals and Labour became the junior partners in the process of government formation. It was the religious parties who would choose to ally with either the left, the right or neither. The election results for this period are presented in Table 7.7.

If the parties are divided into the five categories making up the left–right scale, then the election results become easier to analyse. Figure 7.5 also clearly exhibits the majority constantly held by the dominant and centrally located religious parties, the outdistancing of the moderate right – despite its gains – by the moderate left, and the relative equality of the extreme right and extreme left.

The biggest of the religious parties was the KVP, which had participated in all post-war governments. The second largest was the ARP, which, since 1952, was also consistently represented in government. The smallest religious party, the CHU, was the most conservative of the three and was therefore left out of some coalitions with the PvdA. The PvdA was the bigger of the two non-religious parties. It sought to split the religious parties and govern with as few of them as possible, and thereby make its share of the coalition proportionally larger. The VVD was the alternative partner and usually governed with all three religious parties. The middle position of the religious parties, between the PvdA

Table 7.7 Numerical distribution of Tweede Kamer seats, 1946–63

Party	1946	1948	1952	1956	1959	1963
Pacifist Socialist (PSP)					2	4
Communist (CPN)	10	8	6	7	3	4
Labour (PvdA)	**29**	**27**	**30**	**50**	**48**	**43**
Catholic People's (KVP)	**32**	**32**	**30**	**49**	**49**	**50**
Anti-Revolutionary (ARP)	**13**	**13**	**12**	**15**	**14**	**13**
Christian Historical Union (CHU)	**8**	**9**	**9**	**13**	**12**	**13**
Liberal (VVD)	**6**	**8**	**9**	**13**	**19**	**16**
Farmers' (BP)						3
Reformed Political League (GPV)						1
Reformed Political Party (SGP)	2	2	2	3	3	3
others[a]			1	2		
Total	100	100	100	150	150	150

[a] Catholic National Party, seceded from KVP in 1948 and reunited after 1952 election; parties are listed on a scale from left to right; five major system parties appear in bold; initials in parentheses are the official abbreviations

and the VVD – if one perceives the VVD to be the second major pole of electoral competition – and the electoral dominance of the five major system parties explains why all post-war coalitions have been made up of religious parties with either Labour or the Liberals as alternating coalition partners.

The permanent minority situation that characterized both the PvdA and the VVD forced them to tone down their anti-religious tendencies

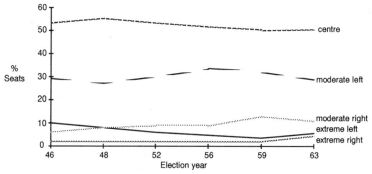

extreme left = Communists (1946–63) + Pacifist Socialist (1959–63)
moderate left = Labour (1946–63)
centre = Catholic People's (1946–63) + Anti–Revolutionaries (1946–63) + Christian Historicals (1946–63)
    + Catholic Nationals (1948–52)
moderate right = Liberals (1946–63)
extreme right = Reformed Political Party (1946–63) + Reformed Political League (1963) + Farmers (1963)

Figure 7.5 Party blocs' percentages of Tweede Kamer seats, 1946–63

in their attempts to court the confessional parties into coalition agreements. The interclass nature of the religious parties – which placed them in the centre of the Dutch political continuum – made a coalition with either moderate left or moderate right a credible option. The other five minor parties – situated both further left than the PvdA and further right than the VVD – were ignored and excluded from this arena. Figure 7.6 presents a graphic representation of the old Dutch party system.

In the second half of the 1960s, the KVP began to experience a rather severe downward spiral in electoral support. The previous exceptional duration and consistency of more than 85 per cent of the Dutch Catholics supporting the KVP rapidly declined to less than half that amount within one decade. The CHU experienced a similar downturn, albeit not as dramatic. The decreasing hold of the religious parties on their voters was directly related to the general process of deconfessionalization and depillarization, which affected The Netherlands at the time. Dissension within the religious pillars led to disorientation, which culminated in an overall disarray of the religious subcultures. Organizational structures which had become part of Dutch tradition began to break apart and fade away.

The stability of the party system also broke down, and new parties appeared at every election. This process had begun previously with the appearance of the Pacifist Socialist Party (PSP) in 1959, and continued with the entrance of the Farmers' Party (BP) and Reformed Political

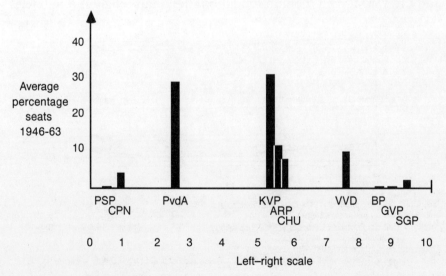

Figure 7.6 The old Dutch party system

League (GPV) in 1963. However, after 1967, the new emerging parties were no longer fringe extremist groups, but moderate and centrist parties that would come to share governing power. The rise of new parties, and their location between the socialist and confessional blocs, is represented in Table 7.8.

The new parties located themselves on the fringes of the major parties, aiming their appeals at the disgruntled voters who could not switch to another pillar. These parties, according to Lijphart

> fit the fourfold bloc pattern of Dutch society. They represent the radical fringes of the blocs: the extreme right of the generally conservative Liberal bloc, the extreme left of the Socialist bloc, and the extremes on both the right and the left of the generally middle-of-the-road Catholic and Calvinist blocs. (Lijphart, 1968: 164)

In the past, the small parties outside the major pillars were ignored and excluded from the consociational process. Since the mid-1960s, however, the new parties have remained oriented towards their pillar of origin – some have even attempted to reconquer it – and they are no longer ignored or excluded from the policy-making arena.

Table 7.8 Numerical distribution of Tweede Kamer seats, 1967–89

Party	1967	1971	1972	1977	1981	1982	1986	1989
Pacifist Socialist (PSP)	4	2	2	1	3	3	1	
Communist (CPN)	5	6	7	2	3	3		6[b]
Radical (PPR)		2	7	3	3	2	2	
Labour (PvdA)	37	39	43	53	44	47	52	49
Democrats '66 (D'66)	7	11	6	8	17	6	9	12
Democratic Socialist (DS'70)		8	6	1				
Catholic People's (KVP)	42	35	27					
Anti-Revolutionary (ARP)	15	13	14	49[c]	48	45	54	54
Christian Historical Union (CHU)	12	10	7					
Liberal (VVD)	17	16	22	28	26	36	27	22
Farmers' (BP)	7	1	3	1				
Reformed Political League (GPV)	1	2	2	1	1	1	1	2
Reformed Political Party (SGP)	3	3	3	3	3	3	3	3
Reformed Political Federation (RPF)					2	2	1	1
Centre (CP)						1		1
others[a]		2	1			1		
Total	150	150	150	150	150	150	150	150

[a] 1971, both seats won by the Middle Class Party; 1972, single seat won by the Roman Catholic Party; 1982, single seat won by the Evangelical People's Party
[b] Green Left, joint list of PSP, CPN and PPR
[c] Christian Democratic Appeal (CDA), merger of KVP, ARP and CHU
Parties are listed on a scale from left to right; five major parties appear in bold; initials in parentheses are the official abbreviations

Table 7.9 Party groups in the new (post-1963) Dutch party system

Extreme left	Moderate left	Centre	Moderate right	Extreme right
PSP, CPN, PPR (from 1977)	PvdA, PPR (till 1972)	D'66, DS'70, CDA (KVP, ARP, CHU)	VVD	BP, GPV, SGP, RPF, CP

The post-1963 Dutch party system can be divided into five major blocs along the left–right political continuum. The parties belonging to each group are presented in Table 7.9.

If the election results are also divided into five categories, then a clearer set of patterns can be exhibited in Figure 7.7: (1) the decline of the centre; (2) the rise of the moderate left; (3) the ascent and descent of the moderate right; and (4) the persistent parity of the extreme right and extreme left.

While the vote of the religious groups was monopolized by their respective parties, the PvdA and VVD were able to compete for the secular vote alone. As the confessional bloc declined, both the moderate left and the moderate right saw the opportunity to win over additional voters. The result was a move from the politics of accommodation to adversarial competition and party system polarization. The upheavals of the 1960s brought about the rapid decay of the old party system. The stability of the old system, based on religious and class determination, eroded and could no longer be sustained in the 1970s. The major system parties were confronted by systemic polarization, and

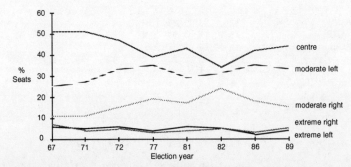

extreme left = Pacifist Socialists (1967–86) + Communists (1967–82) + Radicals (1977–86) + Green Left (1989)
moderate left = Labour (1967–89) + Radicals (1971–73)
centre = Democrats '66 (1967–89) + Democratic Socialists '70 (1971–77) + Catholic People's (1967–72) +
        Anti–Revolutionaries (1967–72) + Christian Historicals (1967–72) + Christian Democrats (1977–89)
moderate right = Liberals (1967–89)
extreme right = Reformed Political League (1967–89) + Reformed Political Party(1967–89) + Farmers' (1967–77) +
        Reformed Political Federation (1981–89) + Centre (1982–89)

Figure 7.7 Party blocs' percentages of Tweede Kamer seats, 1967–89

the newly emerging parties were not linked to religious and class subcultures in the same way as the old ones had been. Moreover, the new parties differed considerably in tactics, perception and ideological inclination from the old parties.

Ultimately, polarization was forsaken and a restoration of the consociational and accommodationist rules of the game was attempted. Furthermore, the major system parties began to regain a larger proportion of parliamentary seats than they had held during the late 1960s and early 1970s. Since 1977, the old party system appears to have reasserted itself. The average parliamentary sizes and spatial location of the parties making up the new Dutch party system are shown in Figure 7.8.

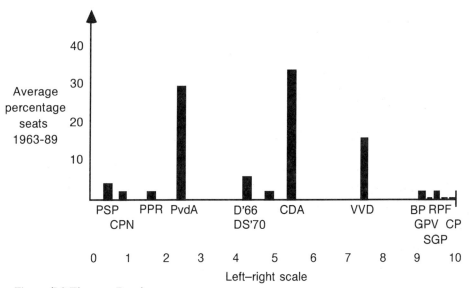

Figure 7.8 The new Dutch party system

Notes

[1] The decline of the Union of the Democratic Centre (UCD) in Spain from 48 per cent of the seats in 1979 to 3 per cent of the seats in 1982, and the rise of polarization from 3.69 to 5.04 (according to this study's polarization measure) in the same time-frame, is an example of just such turbulence which cannot be truly accounted for by the relationship being analysed.

[2] These four representatives are normally not included in calculations as to the relative strength of parties or groups of parties in the Folketing, a convention which this study will adhere to.

[3] Of the 175 members elected from Denmark proper, 135 are elected in constituencies and 40 are supplementary members allocated in a manner so as to ensure

proportionality. This allocation uses the D'Hondt divisor method but applies a modification of the Saint-Laguë method for the divisor. For a party to obtain its share of the seats it must secure at least 2 per cent of the votes in the entire country. For descriptions of the Danish electoral system see Miller (1964), Pedersen (1966), Johansen (1982) and Elklit (1993).

4. Proportional representation was adopted in 1918, replacing a district-based two-ballot electoral system. The country is technically divided into 19 electoral districts, but is effectively one national constituency because parties are allowed to pool votes from different districts. Seats are allocated according to the D'Hondt formula. From the introduction of universal suffrage in 1917 until 1970, voting was compulsory – only since then has non-voting become a legitimate option. Up to 1956, the Tweede Kamer consisted of only 100 seats with no artificial threshold, making it possible for a party to win representation with 1 per cent of the national vote. The country then was tied with Israel, which imposed an artificial 1 per cent threshold for representation in the 120-member Knesset, for the most extreme proportional system in the world. Since the 1956 expansion of the Tweede Kamer to 150 members, the electoral threshold has been effectively lowered to 0.67 per cent, giving The Netherlands the world's undisputed lowest electoral threshold.

8

Unidimensionality, Centre and Extreme Parties

8.1 Adopting Unidimensionality

There seems to be little debate concerning the justified prevalence of a unidimensional left–right model for the old Danish party system. For over a quarter of a century after World War II, Danish politics were thought to lack any of the cleavages which had produced bitter partisan conflicts elsewhere (Pedersen, 1967). Even such minority problems as religion, ethnicity or regionalism did not exist.[1] Moreover, the old Danish party system was characterized by the predominance of left–right debates and terminology. 'The fit with a unilinear model of the political folklore does in fact summarize patterns of legislative behaviour better than more complex models do' (Pedersen, 1987: 11). Surveys of the Danish electorate during that period concluded that 'in spite of indications of multidimensionality, the left–right dimension is by far the most important dimension in the Danish party system' (Elklit *et al.*, 1972: 212). The unidimensional left–right model was also found to be the best explanatory and descriptive tool for understanding not only the relations between parties (Damgaard, 1973), but also the process of government formation (Damgaard, 1969).

The adoption of a unidimensional left–right scale for Denmark until 1973 seems, therefore, to be justified empirically. The debate begins when the post-1973 period is discussed. The social changes manifested in the post-1973 party system, notably the decline in class voting, were indeed dramatic. But were they dramatic enough to alter the basic characteristic of the Danish party system? Abundant literature and research exist which point to a negative answer. The new party system constituted a serious transformation of the old one, but there was an important element of continuity as well. Even those who accept the existence of two dimensions in contemporary Danish politics do not discount the fact that one of these two dimensions is more important than the other. Despite the breakdown of the traditional unidimensional party system, the left–right ordering of parties according to that single dimension was preserved. This continuing dimension still 'explained' 87 per cent of the variance in the party system after 1973 (Damgaard and Rusk, 1976: 185). The second dimension, which appeared in 1973, has been interpreted as one of distrust or discontent, in accordance with the notion that 1973 was a protest election. It has not altered the fact, though, that 'the left–right dimension is still today the principal cleavage dimension in electoral politics. All survey material produced since [1973] documents this continuity' (Pedersen, 1987: 27).

Two studies of Danish party politics both concur that the linear left–right dimension is the most prevalent one, and that it was appropriate for both the old and the new party system. Einhorn and Logue (1988: 163) adopted a model in which 'even the new parties of the 1970s can easily be placed on . . . a single left–right continuum'. Nannestad (1989: 191) concluded that the saliency of a second dimension in the minds of the voters, which he terms the backlash-protest dimension, has diminished since the mid-1970s and that 'it thus appears that the most stable and in general most salient "ideological" dimension in the respondents' perception of the party system in the seventies was the left–right dimension'.

The old Dutch party system, on the other hand, has been viewed as a clear example of the existence of two distinct dimensions: religion and class. Crosscutting religious and class dimensions produced the five political parties that were the representatives of the subcultural pillars that made up Dutch society. Social segmentation along these class lines maintained the pre-1963 'frozen' party system for half a century. As Rose and McAllister (1986: 12) have pointed out, 'The Netherlands has been a classic example of a structured system of multi-party competition, because the electorate has been determined along two dimensions, religion and class, each sustaining separate political parties.'

The post-1963 era has brought about the decline of this structured model, and the party system has become far more open in terms of affiliation, fragmentation and competition (Irwin and van Holsteyn, 1989a, b). This has led to the disappearance of the two-dimensional model, and its replacement by a new, openly competitive, depillarized model which is characterized by a unidimensional, socio-economic, left–right scale. One would, therefore, encounter much less criticism in making a unidimensional argument for the new Dutch party system than one would in making the same case for the old party system. Yet, for the purpose of this study, unidimensionality is adopted for the entire post-war era, and thus a case must be made that a single dimension was appropriate for the old party system during the 1946–63 period as well.

The relative strengths of the socio-economic and religious dimensions can be gauged by testing the coalitions formed over the 1946–90 period, encompassing both the old and the new party systems. Lijphart (1982) argued that when parties can form two different coalitions, each representing a separate dimension, they will tend to form the coalition based on the dimension that is more important to them. The old Dutch party system was made up of five parties that were potential coalition partners. One was a secular left party, another was a secular right party, and the remaining three were religious parties located in the centre of the socio-economic dimension, but set apart from the other two on the religious dimension, as shown in Figure 8.1.

If only alternating centre–right and centre–left coalitions were formed, this would indicate that the socio-economic dimension was the dominant one, because the coalitions minimize the differences on this dimension despite maximizing the differences on the religious

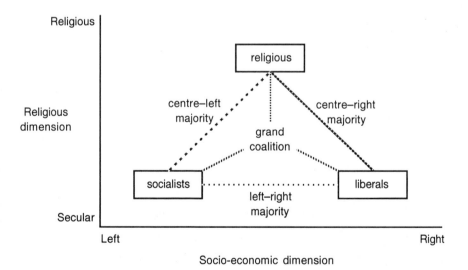

Figure 8.1 Potential governing coalitions in The Netherlands
Adapted from Lijphart (1982)

Table 8.1 Types of government coalition in The Netherlands, 1946–92

Centre–Left	Centre–Right	Left–Right	Left–Centre–Right
40%	51%	0%	9%

dimension. If only left–right coalitions were created, this would show the religious dimension to be dominant, because now the socio-economic differences have been maximized while the religious ones are minimized. If a combination of these two appears, or left–centre–right grand coalitions, then it is impossible to determine which dimension is more salient. The governing coalitions in The Netherlands between 1946 and 1992 are presented in Table 8.1.

The four years of left–centre–right grand coalitions were from 1948 to 1952, and during the following 40 years there have been only centre–left and centre–right coalitions. With a ratio of over 10 to 1, the socio-economic dimension appears to be by far the more salient one. Wolinetz (1974) concurred when he stated that only in the inter-war party system was religion the dominant dimension, producing a continuum with both socialists and liberals at one end and the religious parties at the other. In the post-war party system economic issues have become predominant. The confessional parties are now the centre, and this reorientation is reflected in the pattern of coalitions formed.

Unidimensional party locations have also proven to be the best models for predicting both electoral change and the formation of government coalitions in The Netherlands (van der Eijk and Niemöller, 1985; de Swaan, 1982). The importance of the religious dimension actually diminished even during the days of the old party system, and all parties in the new party system – the confessional ones included – competed with each other along the dominant left–right socio-economic dimension. This clearly means that Dutch party politics since World War II can, and should, be seen as unidimensional.

8.2 Identifying Parties of the Centre

Left–right nomenclature has been in use for over a century in Danish politics. In the early formative years of the party system, the major line of conflict was between the conservative and liberal groups. The former became known as the 'Right' (*Højre*), and the latter assumed the label of 'Left' (*Venstre*). After the rise of the socialist parties, the major cleavage moved left and came to rest between the socialist and bourgeois parties, but the terminology of right and left survived. Modern Danish politics has introduced a third element, the notion of a 'Centre' (*Centrum*). Moderate parties who do not perceive themselves as part of either group, and some of the new small parties as well, describe themselves in terms of being 'left of centre', 'right of centre', or even plain 'centre'.

This study has defined centre to be an ideologically derived positional concept, rather than a spatial location or label (see Chapter 2). The parties of the centre are those along the ideological left–right continuum which occupy the metrical centre or are near it. That is, they are located in the central area of an ideologically defined cross-national space. After the description of the development of the modern Danish party system in Chapter 7, it is clear which parties fall into this category.

A reading of the centre parties' manifestos, or an analysis of their election strategies and coalition behaviour, leads to the uncovering of what is one of the main characteristics of a centre party: all have directed their parliamentary strength towards encouraging successive governments not to make themselves dependent on either extreme of the party spectrum. In other words, not only are the centre parties willing to support either left or right, switching back and forth depending on whichever group is dominant at that point, but this bargaining strategy is bounded by the possibility of parliamentary or governmental co-operation with the extremes.

This pattern was initiated by the Radical Liberals (RV) in the 1960s, which broke away from an alliance with the Social Democrats (SD) when the latter began to co-operate with the extremist Socialist People's Party (SF). The two new parties of the centre, the Centre Democrats (CD) and the Christian People's Party (KRF), were born of protest – the CD against the leftist leanings of the SD, and the KRF in opposition to the liberal policies of the Liberal (V) and Conservative (KF) government – yet both have taken on pragmatic roles in the Folketing, adopting compromising stands on nearly every issue, except extremist tendencies.

> For these parties, it became almost an ideology and a *raison d'être* to compromise and to mediate – a role they could play to the full, in that the distribution of seats in the Folketing required their participation in the formation of any feasible majority. (Bille, 1989: 53)

In short, what truly characterizes the parties of the centre in Denmark is not only their ideological location, but their constant emphasis on the need to reach agreements 'across the centre' and avoid polarization.

The Danish party system is divided by most scholars into five groups, synonymous with the separation of the left–right scale into five categories. This division points to two clear anchors, a socialist moderate left bloc – made up of the SD, one of the most, or even the most, moderate of the European social democratic parties according to most party scales – and a bourgeois moderate right bloc, comprising the V and the KF. Both blocs together have won, on average, approximately three-quarters of the Folketing seats in the post-war era, the moderate left and the moderate right equally averaging about 36–7 per cent. The parties located between these two modes of electoral competition are the middle parties – the RV, CD, KRF and Justice Party (DR). Yet, due to their ideological positions and parliamentary tactics, they are also centre parties. The middle parties and the centre parties in Denmark are, therefore, congruent.

In The Netherlands – now that it has been established that even in the long run the socio-economic, left–right dimension is the main axis of party politics – the confessional parties can be located in the centre of this dimension. This is not to say that religion is centrally located on the left–right scale, but rather that the appeal of the religious parties is both aimed at and attracts a following that is heterogeneous with respect to socio-economic attitudes and status. The consequence is that the interclass religious parties must accommodate themselves to a flexible, and hence centrist, stand on socio-economic issues. Only by locating themselves at the centre of the left–right continuum can the religious parties hope to maintain both their electorate and their influential role. According to Daalder

> The religious parties have a much more heterogeneous social following than either Liberals or Socialists. This has tended to draw the religious parties toward a centrist position and to make them natural brokers between conflicting interests, first within their own ambit, but indirectly also in society at large. (Daalder, 1966: 220)

Irving (1979: 206) took this one step further when he stated that the *raison d'être* of the religious parties is to be 'fulcrum parties of the centre'.

The centre placement of the confessional parties is also due to their history of coalition-making. All three of the religious parties have participated in alternating coalitions with both the Labour Party (PvdA) and the Liberal Party (VVD). None of the religious parties can therefore be placed on the left or right part of the political spectrum. Parties located within either the moderate right or moderate left camps have not participated in government coalitions with members of the opposite camp – unless circumstances placed the country in dire straits and grand coalitions were formed to handle the crisis.

It is important to emphasize that even during the days of the old party system, when the confessional parties held a majority of the seats, they brought in either the PvdA, the VVD, or both at the beginning, into the governing coalition. The only two coalitions between 1946 and 1967 that included only the religious parties were interim cabinets formed to hold upcoming elections. This pattern was based on a desire by the dominant religious party, the Catholic People's Party (KVP), to be able to play off the left and the right within the coalition itself in order to maintain a centrist policy of compromise and consensus.

The merger of the KVP, the Anti-Revolutionary Party (ARP) and the Christian Historical Union (CHU) into the Christian Democratic Appeal (CDA) provides yet a third reason for including the three religious parties in the centre category. The creation of the CDA was the confessional response to the polarization tactics of the PvdA. This strategy was aimed at turning the Dutch party system into a two-bloc bipolar system, providing two clear-cut alternatives for the electorate. The success of this policy would have split the religious voters while forcing the religious parties into the right camp. The formation of the CDA was not only an attempt to counter the electoral decline of the religious parties, but also a decision to cling to the centre. This position had given the confessionals power in the past, and held the potential for continued power in the future even though they had lost their parliamentary majority. According to van Mierlo (1986), the CDA 'refused' to take up a clear position on the left–right dimension, hoping to be able to continue changing coalition partners from left to right and to maintain its dominant central role. The CDA thus became the flag-bearer against the strategy of polarization, and formed a centrist pole of attraction in order to counter this policy.

There were no other parties centrally located during the period of the old party system. The new parties that emerged at the beginning of the new party system located themselves on the edges of the crumbling pillars. Those on the extreme borders of both the liberal and socialist pillars were not candidates for centrality, but those on the right and left of the religious pillar – or, alternatively, on the moderate borders of the liberal and socialist pillars – were. No new party emerged between the confessional and liberal bloc, but two did between the socialist and confessional ones: Democrats '66 (D'66) and the Democratic Socialists (DS'70). The former participated only in religious–socialist coalitions, while the latter took part in only religious–liberal ones. These two parties represent the secular centre-left and centre-right, and both were prepared to enter any government that would pursue their interests. Along with the CDA, D'66 and DS'70 thus made up the centre in the new Dutch party system.[2]

This study has distinguished conceptually between centre and middle parties. Empirically, however, as in Denmark, the two seem to overlap in the Dutch case – but only in the new Dutch party system. In the old party system, the religious parties held a majority of the seats and thus formed one of the two major poles of electoral competition – the socialist PvdA made up the other pole, with an average of almost 30 per cent of the seats. In the new party system, the religious parties lost their majority, and, due to the dramatic increase in seats won by the VVD, the major centre-right pole of competition moved from the religious parties to the VVD. The centre parties in the post-1967 Dutch party system, therefore, came to be located between the two main poles of electoral competition – the PvdA and VVD. In other words, they became middle parties. Yet they also happen to be the ideologically moderate parties, preferring to perform a centrist role.

8.3   Establishing the Extreme Boundary

There are two possible approaches for deciding which parties lay beyond the boundary of extremism: objective and subjective. The former is based on the nature and platform of the party, i.e. the way it objectively perceives itself; the latter is a product of the way that the other parties in the system subjectively construe the party's governing potential, or lack thereof.

The first, objective, approach leads to the conclusion that there were two extremist parties in the post-war Danish party system: the Communist Party (DKP) and the Left Socialists (VS). The DKP's total adherence to both Marxism and the Soviet line clearly placed it in the extremist party category. The VS's split from the SF – in order to combat its moderation and return to, and maybe even surpass, the extremist position of the DKP – made it an appropriate candidate for the extremist label as well. The coalition between the VS and DKP, along with a Marxist–Leninist workers' party which had never been represented in the Folketing, to form the Unity List prior to the 1990 election appears to put this issue to rest. A debate begins when one considers the

SF and the Progress Party (FRP) for membership in the extreme party bloc. It is here that the second, subjective, approach can assist in making the determination.

The SF accepted Marxism as its ideological base. It was anti-capitalist and emphasized public control of and intervention in the economy. It sought to disarm Denmark, and free it from any and all alliances, especially NATO. During the debate and subsequent referendum in Denmark concerning EEC membership, the SF was the only anti-EEC party in the Folketing, wanting to keep Denmark independent of international capitalism. These attributes sufficed to make the SF an extremist party in the eyes of the other consensus-oriented parties. The four old parties, who still dominated the party system, viewed the SF's foreign, economic and social policies as being 'too radical to allow the party to achieve any decisive influence in government' (Borre, 1988: 78). Indeed, the SF was never allotted a cabinet seat, despite the fact that without its participation no socialist majority was ever possible, and with its inclusion alone in a coalition government the SD would have achieved a socialist majority government more than once. Subjectively, therefore, the SF was an extreme left party.

The FRP is a right-wing protest party that has proposed several sensational policies. The party's founder and former long-time leader publicly lauded tax dodgers, calling them heroes and comparing them to railroad saboteurs during the Nazi resistance. Beyond the wish to abolish all taxes and dismantle the armed forces, the party was against continuing any state subsidies to the arts, any foreign aid and the Danish diplomatic service. Moreover, it called for the preservation of the Danish way of life against foreign influences. Its leader was quoted in the 1988 election campaign saying 'So long as there are high taxes and Muslims, we've got something to fight for' (*The Economist*, 28 May 1988: 50).

Furthermore, the party was perceived by all other parties to be a threat to the continuation of Danish political tradition, and has been stigmatized and alienated from parliamentary co-operation.

> The old parties perceived the Progress Party as a threat to the welfare system and to the traditional consensus-oriented party system – as well as to themselves. Hence they treated the Progress Party as an alien in the political society, a party which undermined the legitimacy – not of the constitutional system – but of the vital elements in the welfare system, including the mode of functioning of the political system and the consensus that prevailed among the old parties on this issue. (Bille, 1989: 49–50)

This led the FRP to reconsider its position, and after its leader was jailed there were some moves towards moderation. Nonetheless, the subjective attitude of the other parties had not changed much. Parliamentary support by the FRP was sought by the other parties – as was the backing of the SF – but an open alliance, governmental participation and critical backing on major issues were avoided at all costs. The FRP's threat to the system not only concerned its protest against bureaucracy, taxes and immigration, but also the danger it presented to democracy. Beyond the suggestion of reducing the parliament's size to only 40, it also suggested that royal prerogatives be increased. Support for the FRP has been shown to be based not only on distrust, but also on authoritarian attitudes (Nielsen, 1976). Almost one-half of its voters supported a strong-man seizure of power to solve an economic crisis (Borre, 1977). The FRP was, therefore, subjectively at least, an extremist party outside the 'tradition' of Danish politics, if not 'the most strongly "anti-system" party' (Fitzmaurice, 1981: 118).

The policies of both the SF and the FRP have made these two parties, along with the DKP and the VS, unreliable in terms of *Koalitionsfähigkeit*. These parties were stigmatized and unaccepted as coalition partners, and as a result none participated in government. Scholars have suggested that

> in fact, it is arguably less important in contemporary Scandinavia to establish whether a particular party possesses an anti-system ideology than to note the existence of sizable parties with a low to zero eligibility for governing. While it may be countered that the preclusion from coalitions ... is simply a consequence of their protest character, the 'outcast' status ... carries more serious implications. Obviously, when significant sections of the electorate are denied a voice in government, for whatever reason, this is bound to have a negative feedback effect on levels of popular consent. (Elder *et al.*, 1982: 97)

In other words, even if these parties are not 'anti-system' in their objective outlook, the other parties perceive them as such and treat them as 'system-alienated' parties. The result is that these four extremist parties have affected the party system as if they were anti-system parties – they questioned the regime's legitimacy and undermined its base of support. Since the FRP appeared only in 1973, it would be more precise to say that there were three extremist parties in the old Danish party system, all located on the extreme left, and four in the new party system, encompassing both ends of the scale. It is not coincidental that the tactic of the centre parties was to oppose any government that would be dependent on the FRP on the right, or the VS, DKP and SF on the left.

The two criteria used to distinguish extremist parties in Denmark, objective and subjective extremity, clearly delineate the boundary of extremism in The Netherlands as well. The former criterion, based on the party's nature and platform, reveals four extreme parties. The latter criterion, a result of how the party is subjectively perceived by other parties in the system, reveals four additional extremist parties.

The objective approach uncovers four extremist parties: the Communist Party (CPN) and the Pacifist Socialist Party (PSP) on the extreme left; and the Centre Party (CP) and the Farmers' Party (BP) on the extreme right. The CPN, a strict Marxist–Leninist party, represents the oldest and steadiest opposition on fundamental principles,[3] while the PSP has wavered between revolutionary socialism and radical pacifism. The BP was, in Daalder's (1979: 179) words, 'emphatically anti-system in orientation' based on strong *antidirigiste* and authoritarian feelings, while the CP was a 'controversial ultra-right movement', according to Gladdish (1983: 278), with a philosophy based on xenophobia, racism and fascism. These four parties are thus extremist by the objective definition.

Four additional parties can be included in the extremist category, not because they considered themselves as such, but rather due to the manner in which the moderate and centre parties perceived them: the Radical Party (PPR) on the left; and the Reformed Political League (GPV), the Reformed Political Party (SGP) and the Reformed Political Federation (RPF) on the right. The PPR was, at first, not a candidate for extremity and even participated in government. However, after the 1977 election it abandoned co-operation with the moderate left and joined the ranks of the radical left. Since then it has been excluded from all coalitions. After the 1977 election, which was a landslide for the PvdA, who garnished 10 additional seats (an increase of 23 per cent), the PPR was not even brought into the coalition negotiations, despite the result of these talks which kept the PvdA on the opposition bench. Moreover, the PvdA would have been unable to form a socialist–religious government that included the PPR in its ranks due to the objection of the CDA to having any extremists in power. The 1989 merger of the CPN, PSP and PPR into the Green Left provides the final step in its movement from the moderate left to subjective radicalism, and finally to objective extremity. Not only the moderate parties perceive the PPR to be extremist; those parties on the radical left now see it as part of their camp, and its own self-perception has become that of an extreme left party.

The three small orthodox religious parties to the right of the VVD –

the GPV, SGP and RPF – can also be placed in the extremist group, according to the subjective definition. Despite the fact that, when the CDA and VVD were just short of a majority, one or more of these parties would have made a majority coalition possible, they have yet to be brought into coalition negotiations and have never sat in government. With purely doctrinal demands upon which no compromise is acceptable, such as legislation in conformity with the Bible, these parties have destined themselves to constant isolation. The VVD, which during and after the polarization period attempted to become a mass party, has been unable, or unwilling, to share power with these parties. They are, therefore, part of the extreme right category.

In short, the eight extremist parties of the Dutch party system can be characterized either by ideological extremity or by subjective isolation from government potential by the governing-oriented parties – i.e. permanent opposition status. Moreover, the accommodationist principles of Dutch politics are threatened by these parties, which adds to the alienation that the moderate parties feel towards the extremes. The result is that the Dutch party system has always possessed extreme parties both on its right and on its left. Between 1946 and 1956, the CPN and the SGP were the only two extreme parties; in 1959, the PSP joined; in 1963, both the GPV and the BP appeared; since 1977, the PPR could be included as well; in 1981, the RPF was added; and in 1982, the CP emerged. After the quick decline of the CPN in the post-war years, the two extremes have been relatively stable and of equal size. Although they did not participate in government, or have a decisive impact on Dutch politics, they were able to mobilize discontent and encroach on the electorate of the governing parties.

Even though Denmark had only four extreme parties, as opposed to eight in The Netherlands, its extreme parties were larger. The ratio was relatively even between the two countries during the period of the old party systems, but in the new party systems the Danish extremes rose to double the average size of their more numerous Dutch counterparts.

Notes

[1.] Only three regional minorities have achieved representation in the Folketing: the two representatives each of the Faroe Islands and Greenland, and the representative of the German minority (Slesvig Party) from 1953 to 1964. All five have by and large avoided direct intervention in Danish politics, except in matters concerning their electorate. In other words, the Danish minority representatives have upheld an attitude of neutrality *vis-à-vis* the balance of power between the Danish parties.

[2.] This in-depth result, which defines the CDA, D'66 and DS'70 as centre parties in

The Netherlands, corresponds exactly to the earlier, rather arbitrary, boundary surrounding the centre which was used by the statistical analysis for the generation of the model – all parties that fall between 4 and 6 on the left-right scale.

3. As an example of the isolation that the major system parties imposed on the CPN, known members were disqualified from most types of government employment, and communists were not acceptable even as local government partners; they were also excluded from certain parliamentary committees, and were not allotted time on radio or television.

9

A Static Exploration

9.1 Centre and Extreme Parties in the Danish Party System

Now that the theoretical, methodological, statistical and descriptive groundwork has been prepared, the two explanations proposed in the model for the apparent lack of a relationship between the parliamentary strength of the centre parties and the level of party system polarization can be tested across time, and not just cross-nationally. Each explanation will be analysed in both countries, beginning with the explanation that argues that there is a relationship between the centre parties' share of parliamentary seats and that of the extreme parties. Chapter 10 will evaluate the explanation that suggests a relationship between the centre's parliamentary strength and the movement of the moderate parties along the left–right scale. In short, now that cross-national empirical support for both explanations has been shown, these two chapters set out to test the explanations in depth with evidence from two case studies. The goal is to uphold one of the two explanations as the more valid relationship in the model.

The statistical analysis condensed the original 10 points of the left–right continuum into five categories. Due to the relative stability of parties in Denmark along this scale, it is difficult to encounter a party that has crossed the threshold between one category and another, even after more than four decades of policy changes and election strategies since World War II. That is, a moderate left party, such as the Social Democrats (SD), might have become more centre-oriented at some period, or quite left-leaning at another period. However, the SD cannot be said to have ever been a party of the centre, or one of the extreme left. This is true for all of the parties analysed in Denmark. Since the statistical analyses regress one category against another, rather than specific parties, the movement of a specific party within a particular category will not impact on the results. Therefore, the classification of parties into categories produces an extremely stable measure over an extended period of time. In summary, the use of categories as the basis of analysis allows for the expansion of the applicability of the left–right scale adopted to cover most of the post-war period, and thus enables the research to cover all 18 Danish elections from 1947 to 1988.

The empirical evidence from post-war Denmark validates the under-lying assumptions resulting from the cross-national statistical analysis: when the moderate and the centre parties' shares of parliamentary seats are correlated, the result is a negative correlation, $r = -0.522$;[1] the moderate and the extreme parties' shares of parliamentary seats also produce a strong negative correlation, $r = -0.868$.[2]

If the first explanation for the lack of a relationship between the parliamentary strength of centre parties and the level of party system polarization – which argues that there is a positive relationship between centre and extreme parties' parliamentary shares of seats in the large centre category alone – is to be validated by the Danish case, then no correlation between the parliamentary strength of centre parties and the level of party system polarization should exist, and nor should there be a correlation between the parliamentary strengths of centre and extreme parties, because Denmark represents the small centre parties' category. Regression analysis indeed produces no relationship between the parliamentary strength of centre parties and the level of party system polarization in Denmark for all elections between 1947 and 1988. The correlation coefficient is very small, and statistically insignif-icant[3] – the expected result. A scatterplot of these results is presented in Figure 9.1.

A correlation of centre and extreme parties' shares of seats also does not exhibit a significant result,[4] thereby alluding to no relationship, as is apparent from Figure 9.2 – again, the result expected.

Figure 9.1 showed that while the parliamentary strength of the centre parties fluctuated between 6 per cent and 22 per cent of the seats – more than a 350 per cent increase – the level of party system polariza-tion formed a horizontal cluster around a mean of 3.7 (much like the one in Figure 3.3 covering all the countries in this study). There is no apparent positive or negative slope which can be seen, but rather a flat horizontal cluster signifying no relationship between the independent and dependent variables.

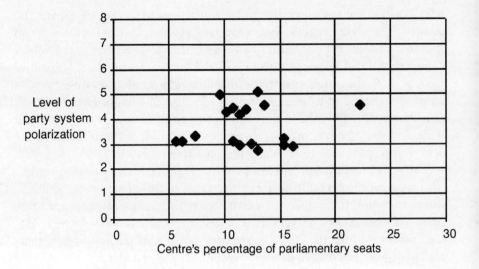

Figure 9.1 Centre parties with polarization in Denmark, 1947–88

However, a closer look at Figure 9.1 will show two separate clusters and one outlier. There appears to be one series of cases clustered along a rather low level of systemic polarization while another series is clustered around a higher level. The first is found on or near a systemic

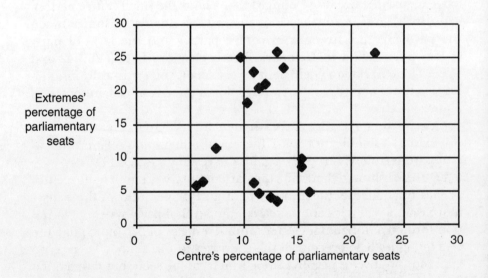

Figure 9.2 Centre parties with extreme parties in Denmark, 1947–88

polarization level of 3, while the second is spread out between 4 and 5 on the polarization scale. The outlier is the only election that surpasses the 20 per cent threshold for centre party seats.

An analysis of these two clusters produces an interesting result. All ten cases in the lower cluster are elections that were classified as the 'old' Danish party system – from 1947 to 1971. The outlier is the peculiar 'earthquake' election of 1973. The remaining seven cases in the top cluster belong to what was called the 'new' Danish party system – since 1975 (see Chapter 7). Within each cluster there is no apparent trend concerning the centre parties' parliamentary strength – it rises and falls randomly. The level of systemic polarization, on the other hand, is maintained at a reasonably constant level by the cases in each separate cluster, as Figure 9.3 shows.

It is interesting to note that the mean percentage of centre parties' seats for both clusters is almost equivalent – 11.4 per cent for the old Danish party system and 11.6 per cent for the new Danish party system – whereas the mean level of systemic polarization is 50 per cent larger in the second cluster – 3.02 for the old Danish party system and 4.55 for the new Danish party system. This leads to the conclusion that the mean level of party system polarization rose from one period to the next despite the fairly constant share of centre parties' seats over time, indicating that there is no relationship between these two variables.

The only connection between the parliamentary strength of the centre parties and the level of systemic polarization is found in the

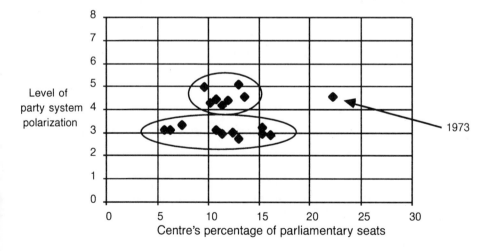

Figure 9.3 Clusters of centre parties with polarization in Denmark, 1947–88

results of the 1973 election. This deviant election shattered the framework of the old Danish party system and exhibited an increase both in the parliamentary strength of the centre parties and in the level of party system polarization. It thus appears that the most anomalous case is the only one that shows a positive relationship between the independent and dependent variables. Within two years a new election reversed the direction of this relationship by not only maintaining but actually increasing the level of systemic polarization, while the centre parties lost more than half of their seats in parliament.

Apart from the volatile and temporary aberration of 1973, Denmark appears to validate the first part of the first explanation – when the centre is small there is no linear relationship between the centre parties' share of parliamentary seats and the level of party system polarization. The Danish case shows an increase in the mean level of systemic polarization between two time periods that is, therefore, not related to the parliamentary strength of centre parties. The reason for the rise in the mean polarization score for the second cluster is apparently the appearance of an extreme right party in a hitherto vacant category. The old Danish party system possessed parties on the extreme left, but none on the extreme right. The new Danish party system has parties in all five categories along the left–right ideological continuum. A breakdown of party categories for both the old and the new Danish party systems presented in Table 9.1 supports this conclusion.

In summary, the first explanation of the constant level of party system polarization despite the increase in the centre parties' share of parliamentary seats – a positive relationship between centre and extreme parties only for those countries with a large centre – is supported empirically by the Danish case. Denmark, as the chosen case study of a country with a small centre, exhibits all of the assumed underlying negative relationships between centre and moderate parties as well as

Table 9.1 Mean centre, moderate and extreme parties' seat percentage and level of systemic polarization in Denmark broken down by period

Category	Period 1 Old party system	Period 2 New party system
Centre parties	11.4	11.6
Moderate parties	79.3	65.7
Extreme parties	6.5	22.4
Polarization	3.0	4.6

between moderate and extreme parties. The expected lack of a relationship between centre and extreme parties in the small centre category, along with no relationship between centre parties and polarization, is also manifested by the empirical evidence from the Danish case.

9.2 Centre and Extreme Parties in the Dutch Party System

The condensing of the original 10 points into five categories, and the relative stability of the Dutch parties along the left–right continuum (with the single exception of the Radical Party, PPR), allow this study to cover all 14 Dutch elections between 1946 and 1989, similar to the Danish case. As Andeweg (1982: 206) concluded, 'there has been a remarkable stability in the Left–Right placement of the parties'. Van der Eijk and Niemöller agreed, stating that

> the party space evinces a considerable stability as to the ordering and relative positioning of the parties. Very few parties surpass other ones in one direction or another, and if they do so, they were, and remain exceedingly close together. (Van der Eijk and Niemöller, 1983: 254)

If the first explanation is to be validated also by the Dutch case, there should be a positive relationship between the parliamentary strengths of centre and extreme parties – because The Netherlands represents the large centre parties' category – impacting positively on the level of party system polarization.

The Netherlands, like Denmark, validates the underlying assumptions resulting from the cross-national statistical analysis. When the moderate and centre parties' shares of parliamentary seats are correlated, the result is a strongly negative correlation, $r = -0.938$.[5] The moderate and extreme parties' shares of parliamentary seats also produce a negative, but not quite statistically significant, correlation, $r = -0.438$.[6]

However, regression analysis for all of the elections between 1946 and 1989 in The Netherlands produces a different relationship than the one expected between the parliamentary strength of centre parties and the level of party system polarization. The correlation coefficient is strongly negative, not positive: $r = -0.690$.[7] A scatterplot of the results is presented in Figure 9.4.

A correlation of centre and extreme parties' shares of seats also does not exhibit the expected positive relationship, and instead produces no relationship whatsoever,[8] as Figure 9.5 shows. This is similar to the

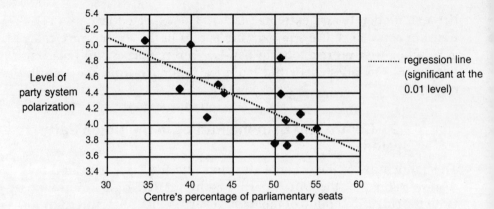

Figure 9.4 Centre parties with polarization in The Netherlands, 1946–89

result from the Danish case study which represented the small centre category, and not what the statistical analysis leads us to believe would be the relationship in the case study chosen from the large centre category.

A further analysis of Figure 9.4 shows that the election results can be classified according to year, similar to the Danish case. Six of the seven cases found in a cluster at the bottom right-hand corner of the scatterplot belong to what was termed the 'old' Dutch party system – from 1946 to 1963. The six cases more to the left and nearer to the top left-hand corner of the scatterplot, plus the one remaining case from the previous cluster, are the elections which were classified as the 'new'

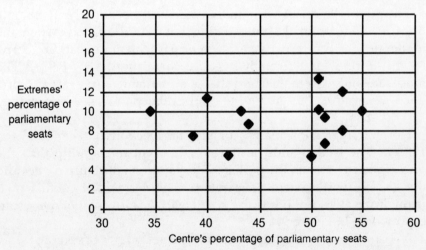

Figure 9.5 Centre parties with extreme parties in The Netherlands, 1946–89

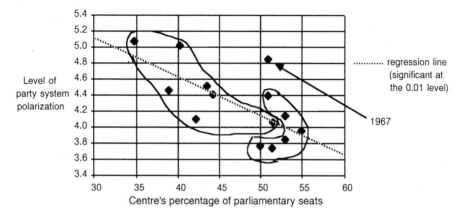

Figure 9.6 Clusters of centre parties with polarization in The Netherlands, 1946–89

Dutch party system – since 1971. The most deviant case from the regression line, found in the top right-hand corner, is the destabilizing election of 1967 which put an end to the old party system. These two groups, and the single outlier, are shown in Figure 9.6.

Within each group there is an entirely different mean seat percentage of the centre parties and mean level of systemic polarization. The old party system's mean percentage of centre party seats is significantly higher than that of the new party system – 52.1 per cent versus 41.9 per cent – whereas the old party system's mean level of polarization is much lower than that of the new party system – 3.96 as opposed to 4.51. This leads to the conclusion that the new party system has incurred a loss of parliamentary seats by the centre parties and a simultaneous rise in systemic polarization. Once again, this is exactly the opposite relationship to that which we expected to encounter based on the cross-national statistical analysis.

The Dutch case thus shows an increase in the mean level of systemic polarization between two time periods which appears to be negatively related to the parliamentary strength of the centre parties. Unlike the Danish case, the reason for the growth of systemic polarization in the new Dutch party system is not an increase in the extreme parties' share of parliamentary seats. The mean seat percentage of the extreme parties is quite stable between the old and the new party system – 8.7 per cent for the former and 8.9 per cent for the latter.

The centre parties, therefore, must have lost most of their seats to the moderate parties – this explains the extremely strong and significant negative correlation between these two categories and the increase in the level of party system polarization. The almost equivalent exchange

Table 9.2 Mean centre, moderate and extreme parties' seat percentage and level of systemic polarization in The Netherlands broken down by period

Category	Period 1 Old party system	Period 2 New party system
Centre parties	52.1	41.9
Moderate parties	39.2	48.9
Extreme parties	8.7	8.9
Polarization	4.0	4.5

of seats between these two categories, while the extreme parties remain almost constant, is depicted in Table 9.2, based on mean shares of parliamentary seats in the old and new Dutch party systems.

In summary, The Netherlands, as the chosen case study of a country with a large centre, exhibits practically all of the assumed underlying relationships that the statistical analysis uncovered for this category, between centre and moderate parties as well as between moderate and extreme parties. However, the expected relationship between centre and extreme parties, and any relationship between centre parties and party system polarization, are not found. Instead, an insignificant relationship is found between centre and extreme parties, which does not impact positively on the level of systemic polarization. The rise in the level of party system polarization is due entirely to the outward flow of seats between the centre and moderate parties. A strong and significant negative relationship thus exists between the centre parties' share of parliamentary seats and the level of party system polarization.

The first explanation, in the model of the relationship between the parliamentary strength of the centre parties and the level of party system polarization, argues that there is a positive correlation between the strengths of centre and extreme parties, in those cases with a large centre. The analysis of the Danish case, where a small centre is supposed to have no relationship with the extreme parties, supports the model. In the Dutch case, however, where a large centre should have a positive relationship with the extreme parties, no such relationship was found. Thus, the model has been substantiated on its less significant assertion, but the more consequential claim is not confirmed. The first explanation is, therefore, invalidated by the case studies.

The second, alternative explanation in the model resulting from the cross-national statistical analysis, based on shifts in party positions, is tested in these same two cases in Chapter 10.

Notes

1. $R^2 = 0.272$; $b = -1.270$; significant at the 0.05 level.
2. $R^2 = 0.753$; $b = -0.805$; significant at the 0.01 level.
3. $r = 0.152$; $R^2 = 0.023$; $b = 0.032$; significant $t = 0.546$.
4. $r = 0.237$; $R^2 = 0.056$; $b = 0.534$; significant $t = 0.345$.
5. $R^2 = 0.879$; $b = -1.039$; significant at the 0.01 level.
6. $R^2 = 0.192$; $b = -0.147$; significant $t = 0.117$. However, due to the small number of cases (N = 14) and to a rather clear pattern exhibited by a scatterplot of the results, this correlation cannot be ignored and should be taken into consideration.
7. $R^2 = 0.476$; $b = -0.048$; significant at the 0.01 level.
8. $r = 0.104$; $R^2 = 0.011$; $b = 0.039$; significant $t = 0.724$.

10

A Dynamic Investigation

10.1 Centre and Moderate Parties in the Danish Party System

The ability of the measures to test the second alternative explanation is somewhat circumscribed. The same characteristic that made it possible to use a mapping of parties generated in the early 1980s for almost the entire post-war period also serves as a liability in attempting to assess the validity of the second explanation, which posits that there is a relationship between a rise in strength of the centre parties and an outward movement of the moderate parties.

The left–right scale of party locations is a static one, and does not allow for party movement along the continuum. Once a party has been located at a specific point along the scale, it remains there. However, at this stage, the movement of parties assumes the highest level of significance. If the Danish Social Democrats (SD), for example, changed from being a centre-leaning moderate left party to one that is courting the extreme left – and this is the crux of the second explanation – the measures will not be able to pick this up. The only alternative is to check the movement of voters between two parties within one category, thereby assessing the radicalization or moderation of the entire category. However, this cannot be accomplished if there is only one party within the category, which is the case for at least two of the five categories in the Danish party system, and at times for more than just two categories. The solution is to assess the movement of parties along the scale based on scholarly literature and empirical analysis.

At this phase it is necessary to examine indicators that would show either a centripetal or a centrifugal movement of parties. The second explanation uncovered by the cross-national statistical findings points to the centrifugal movement of the moderate parties as the major reason for an increase in systemic polarization. The in-depth static analysis of Denmark in Chapter 9 showed that just such an increase in polarization took place when the Danish party system was transformed from the old to the new constellation. However, it was the appearance of an extreme right party that caused this increase in systemic polarization, not another category – i.e. the centre.

Could systemic polarization that was missed by the measures have taken place in Denmark during the post-war period? In other words, did the moderate parties introduce a centrifugal trend which began the pattern of polarization prior to the appearance of a new party on the extreme right? A positive answer to this would mean that the emergence of the Progress Party (FRP) in 1973 on the extreme right is not the cause of the rise in systemic polarization, but a consequence of it.

The second explanation, above and beyond placing the blame for exacerbated systemic polarization on the moderate parties, further argues that the extreme parties have either no influence, or maybe even a negative one, on the level of polarization. The Danish data lend support to this explanation.

When the Socialist People's Party (SF) broke off from the Communist Party (DKP) in 1958, it not only presented a more temperate version of an extreme left party, but also totally replaced the DKP in the Folketing. Later, when the DKP regained representation in parliament and another ultra-left party, the Left Socialists (VS), was established in opposition to the more restrained SF, this represented a re-radicalization of the extreme left parties. However, both the DKP and the VS failed to survive for more than several elections, and most of their seats were captured by the more restrained SF. The trend of the extreme left is therefore a rather stable, if somewhat rising, percentage of parliamentary seats coupled with both centrifugal and centripetal trends – but the latter is prevalent over the former. In short, the overall influence of the extreme left on party system polarization has not been positive, despite the failed attempt by the ultra-left to further polarize the party system.

The extreme right has shown a slightly different pattern. Up until 1973, it hardly existed. The extreme right Independents' Party (U), which split from the Liberals (V) in the mid-1950s, failed to gain parliamentary representation at first, and then held 3 per cent of the seats for only two elections before ceasing to exist. The momentous appearance of the FRP in 1973, with 16 per cent of the parliamentary seats, truly established the presence of an extreme right party. However, its share of seats decreased over time and its position moved in a centripetal pattern. The result is that the extreme right had a dramatically positive influence on the level of systemic polarization in 1973, but has since continuously decreased its impact.

Overall, it appears as though the extreme parties had both offsetting negative and positive influences on systemic polarization during the period of the old party system. In 1973, the extreme parties had an abrupt, forceful and substantial positive impact on the level of party system polarization, only to be followed by an immediate resumption of the previous pattern of offsetting influences in the new party system – albeit at a now higher level of systemic polarization. This conclusion is similar to the one reached by the static analysis. The question that needs to be answered now is: did the moderate right or moderate left parties exhibit the assumed centre-fleeting pattern which would produce an escalated level of party system polarization?

Empirical analysis appears to support this assumption. The formation of the SF on the extreme left helped bring about a 'workers'' majority in the Folketing for the first time after the 1966 election. The SF and SD together held 89 of the 175 parliamentary seats. The SF represented an extreme left which was now both more powerful and more moderate, and could therefore no longer be maintained in a political ghetto by the moderate left. The SF was, therefore, able to put an end to the ostracism of the extreme left which had doomed it to be looked upon as untouchable when it came to government formation. The SD thus decided to reverse its previous policy of not collaborating with the extreme left, and moved leftwards in order to co-operate with the SF. A full-fledged coalition was still unlikely, but the two parties formed a 'contact committee' and began close yet informal parliamentary co-operation on domestic policy. The SF was even offered seats in the so-called 'Red Cabinet', which it decided not to accept.

In 1967, a group within the SF, who opposed any collaboration with the moderate left, split and founded the more radical VS, thereby removing the majority held by the SF and SD for just over a year. After a new election was held in 1968, a centre-right coalition of Radical Liberals (RV), Liberals (V) and Conservatives (KF) was formed. These parties lost their majority in the subsequent 1971 election and were replaced by a second minority SD government, with support from the SF. Once again this informal coalition was undermined by a split, this time in the SD. The break came from those who opposed further collaboration with the extreme left, and it established the centrist Centre Democrats (CD).

The possibility of an amalgamated socialist bloc, which would rely on extremist support, was anathema to the centrist RV. It was forced to ally with the two 'bourgeois' parties in an attempt to undermine the minority SD government supported by the extremist SF. But, simultaneously with the outward movement of the moderate left, the moderate right also exhibited a centrifugal trend. In the early 1960s, the V moved closer to its more reactionary partner in the moderate right category, the KF. Discussions concerning a closer alliance and even possibly a fusion took place, but were never realized.

This outward movement brought about the creation of a group within the V, Liberal Debate, to combat such a move. By 1965, this group broke off from the V to form a separate party, Liberal Centre (LC), which managed to gain representation in the subsequent 1966 election, but lost it thereafter. The leader of the V, who stood for close co-operation with the KF, resigned and was replaced by a leader who opposed amalgamation with the KF, preferring a closer relationship with the centrist RV and thereby moving the V away from its proximity to the KF. The 1968 election placed these three parties in government, and forced the KF to gravitate towards the centre in order to co-operate with the now centre-leaning V and the centrist RV. The supporters of the KF expected to see their party reverse the policies of the welfare state, but were disappointed. In response they punished their party in the 1971 election, when the KF lost the largest proportion of seats since 1947, and then halved its representation again in the subsequent 1973 election. The centripetal trend was immediately reversed, and the KF moved back to its original ideological position.

The leftward movement of the SD, and the rightward movement of both the RV and V, and subsequently the KF as well, almost brought about the formation of a two-bloc party system in Denmark. Fitzmaurice (1981: 122) wrote that 'Denmark was moving towards, if not a two-party system, a two-bloc system on a classic right–left alignment'. Borre (1980: 247) agreed, stating that 'when the Socialist People's Party [SF] in 1966 grew to the status of a regular fifth member of the party system, a two-bloc system with a clear socialist–nonsocialist cleavage resulted'.

Pedersen *et al.* (1971) have shown that a centrifugal movement of parties did indeed take place, more than just once, in the post-war Danish party system prior to the 1973 election. Already in the early 1950s, the gap between the moderate left and the moderate right began to grow, and it reached substantial proportions by the late 1950s. This distance then receded, only to widen once more in the late 1960s, as described above. These findings are corroborated by Holmstedt and Schou (1987: 199–206), who attempted to chart the movement of parties over time along the left–right scale based on an analysis of party manifestos. The authors concluded that the moderate left, the SD, and the moderate right, the V and KF, moved away from each other in the late 1950s, and once again in the late 1960s and early 1970s, while the centrist RV maintained an almost constant middle position during the entire post-war period.

It thus appears that the polarization of the Danish party system had its roots in the 1960s. The centrifugal movement of both moderate right and moderate left parties, not to mention the centre party, created the openings which were filled in the tumultuous election of 1973: (1) a right-leaning centre which left an unoccupied centre-left; (2) a less radical extreme left which opened up the ultra extreme left; and (3) a still vacant extreme right. This election served notice that the Danish voters were not only dissatisfied with the existing parties, but were also opposed to the two-bloc constellation which was emerging. The parties took notice, and within a relatively short time the tripolar left–centre–right pattern of interaction was reinstated.

Immediately after the 1973 election, the leaders of the major parties realized that their mistaken tactics had brought on not only volatility but instability as well. The spectrum of possible coalition partners was, once again, shortened to exclude the extreme right and extreme left parties. Both moderate right and moderate left party leaders recognized the limitations of coalition-making, and their need to govern with the centre. The ensuing government was based solely on the V, with less than 13 per cent of the parliamentary seats, which built *ad hoc* legislative coalitions with each party that was willing to offer support. The 1975 election produced another single-party minority government, this time based on the SD, which courted similar legislative coalitions. The emerging pattern was co-operation across the centre.

The moderate parties had come to acknowledge several factors: (1) they would not be able to build a majority on their own; (2) they could not govern with their extremist neighbours without incurring a backlash; and (3) co-operation across the centre was, therefore, essential. The logic of these factors brought about a *rapprochement* between the SD and the V, who together formed a coalition after the 1977 election, thereby signifying an end to their strategy of polarization and the adoption of a centripetal trend. This government severely strained both parties, and the coalition broke up a year later.

The inability of moderate left or moderate right parties to pass the threshold of majority status and gain control of government would appear to have led them to adopt a strategy of polarizing the party system in order to either destroy the centre, or to force the centre to ally with one of the two sides on a permanent basis – in either case the outcome is the transformation of a tripolar configuration into a two-bloc constellation. These attempts failed to achieve their desired goal, but they did undermine the foundation of the post-war Danish party system, manifested in the 1973 election.

The conclusion from the Danish case study is that despite the rather small size of the centre's share of parliamentary seats, polarizing tendencies were present and did impact on the party system. Moreover, these tendencies were initiated by the moderate parties. In the Danish case they resulted in the emergence of radical parties on both extremes of the party system, and diminished the parliamentary strength of the central core made up of moderate and centre parties. Not only did the strategy of polarization not bear any of its desired fruits, but it eventually made centre-based coalition-making a more difficult and onerous task both mathematically – the increased difficulty in reaching a majority coalition – and governmentally – the larger number of coalition partners necessary. Denmark thus lends support to the second explanation as well – centrifugal trends caused by the moderate parties which impact positively on systemic polarization can be found in a country with a small centre.

In summary, despite the lack of a relationship between the centre parties' share of parliamentary seats and the level of party system polarization in those countries with small centres, the existence of a centre appeared to have motivated the moderate parties to become the culprits for introducing polarizing tendencies. These strategies of polarization turned out to be unsuccessful and were terminated, but they had a lasting impact on the party system.

10.2 Centre and Moderate Parties in the Dutch Party System

The in-depth static analysis of The Netherlands in Chapter 9 showed that the level of polarization did increase as the centre parties lost seats to the moderate parties. This outward flow of seats should impact positively on the measure of polarization. However, there is a question that the second explanation raises: did the moderate parties not only gain seats but also move outwards at the same time, thereby magnifying their positive impact on the level of party system polarization in The Netherlands? The answer is unequivocally affirmative.

The early 1970s saw the introduction of a clear-cut strategy of polarization initiated by the socialist Labour Party (PvdA). The PvdA was among the weakest of the European socialist parties, and had always faced a bloc of religious parties that straddled the centre and held a majority in parliament. The PvdA, much like the Liberals (VVD), ended up as the junior partner in whatever coalition it was invited to join. Moreover, the religious parties usually played off the PvdA against the VVD, eliciting numerous concessions in exchange for participation in government.

When the confessional parties fell below the majority threshold for the first time in 1967, both the PvdA and the VVD saw the opportunity to achieve electoral gains. The breakdown of what had until then been an unassailable religious majority, coupled with an ongoing process of deconfessionalization, motivated both the PvdA and the VVD alike to compete for the available voters in the centre. Their strategy, more so that of the PvdA, due to its much larger size than the VVD, was not to move centripetally and court the centre voters, but to move centrifugally and destroy the centre parties. Irwin stated that

> as the decline of the religious parties set in, the Socialists and Liberals found themselves joined in a common strategy of attempting to win over those voters who were leaving the confessional fold. This has led to a heightened polarisation of Dutch politics. (Irwin, 1980: 216)

A short-lived attempt at a centripetal strategy was tried, but quickly discarded. Immediately after the 1967 election, the PvdA hoped either to establish a long-term alliance with the Anti-Revolutionary Party (ARP), or for a split in the Catholic People's Party (KVP). The former never materialized, and the latter created the Radical Political Party (PPR) in 1968, which proved too weak to provide the socialists with a majority. The centripetal approach was subsequently abandoned, largely for two reasons: Schmelzer's Night and New Left. The former took place in October 1966, when the KVP dropped the PvdA from the coalition in mid-term, and continued to govern with the parliamentary backing of the VVD. The ensuing election in 1967 produced a formal coalition between the religious and liberal parties. The betrayal of the PvdA by the KVP made further close co-operation unlikely, and stirred up a group within the PvdA which crystallized into a faction called New Left. This faction was composed of militant socialists who sought to create a popular front with the parties of the extreme left – the

Communist Party (CPN) and the Pacifist Socialist Party (PSP). It would be several years before they gained practical control of the PvdA, but their influence could not be restrained and helped to bring about the quick demise of the centripetal tactics. The growing strength of New Left had an additional effect in that it alienated many moderate socialists, who then split from the PvdA and spurred the formation of Democratic Socialists '70 (DS'70), which intended to continue the moderate line abandoned by PvdA. This left the PvdA in the hands of New Left and its allies. This faction, according to Irwin and van Holsteyn (1989a: 112), 'instead of resigning itself to the rules of the "politics of accommodation" set upon a policy of polarisation'.

The VVD, which also held hopes for an exclusive majority, began to consider turning for support to the fundamentalist parties of the extreme right. However, due to the large gap between the combined seats of both the right and extreme right parties, and a parliamentary majority, the VVD had to tread much more softly. The VVD also stood to gain from the growing alienation between the PvdA and confessionals, because it was now the only likely coalition partner for the religious parties. But the VVD also wanted to capture the available centre voters, and thus adopted a tactic of convincing former confessional voters that only a vote for the VVD could prevent the re-emergence of a religious–socialist coalition. The VVD, therefore, also took part in the centrifugal trend based on a strategy of polarization, but it could not afford to attack the religious parties as openly as the PvdA did. The VVD thus deliberately sought to broaden its appeal to include not only middle-class and religious liberals, but conservative voters who supported the extreme right and voters in general who were opposed to socialism. The VVD used the polarization tactics of the PvdA as a contrast to its own positions and became more of a mass party.

By the early 1970s, the PvdA's party executive had fallen to New Left, and resolutions committing the party to more leftist policies and forbidding a coalition with the KVP were passed. Stringent attacks on the religious–liberal cabinet were mounted, which culminated just prior to the 1971 election when the PvdA, PPR and Democrats '66 (D'66) formed a progressive alliance and presented a programme along with a slate of ministers. The focus of this polarization strategy was to shift from *parliamentary* to *electoral* politics. Instead of the parliamentary parties forming a coalition based on opportunism – which included the switching of coalition partners without an election – the parties would agree on coalition partners *prior* to the election and offer the electorate a clear choice. It was implicit in this strategy that the religious parties would become part of the right bloc. The result would be a two-bloc system, where all the non-bourgeois religious voters would defect to the progressive bloc. The same alliance presented itself when the centre-right cabinet fell and a new election was called in 1972. The PvdA also sought support from the extremist PSP and CPN, which had already helped it form exclusively left coalitions in some city governments. D'66, which at that point was either equivalent in parliamentary strength or larger than the two extremist parties, refused to incorporate these parties and they were left out.

Both the 1971 and 1972 elections brought gains for the PvdA. The 1972 election also saw the VVD win additional seats. The religious parties' share of seats declined in both elections. Daalder stated:

> Socialists and Liberals thus became tacit allies in a non-zero sum electoral game at the expense of the religious parties. Although they remained dependent on a post-election coalition with the religious parties for the formation of cabinets, they had every incentive to polarize the vote at election time. (Daalder, 1979: 185)

The religious parties had come to the point where they faced competition for their previously stable electorate from both sides. After the elections, the progressive bloc had declared its common manifesto unalterable, while the religious parties and the VVD were far below a majority. Inter-party negotiations on the formation of a government thus became deadlocked. Numerically it was impossible for a coalition to be formed without the PvdA or the religious parties, but due to the electoral tactics that the parties had adopted this took an unprecedented 164 days to negotiate.

The new Dutch government was made up of the PvdA, PPR, D'66, KVP and ARP. The progressive parties held ten ministries, while the religious parties were allotted only six. The severing of the Christian Historical Union (CHU), which remained in the opposition, from the other two religious parties in government pushed forward the socialist hopes that a split could be orchestrated between the left-oriented confessionals and their more conservative brethren. The result was exactly the opposite. The inferior status that the ARP and KVP received in the socialist–religious coalition provided the impetus for the three religious parties to begin discussions on joining forces in future elections. The two religious parties in the cabinet held 41 seats, as opposed to the 55 held by the three progressive parties. But the confessionals' share of ministries was below their proportion in the coalition. Had the CHU not remained outside, the religious parties would have held 48 seats, and would have been able to demand increased ministerial representation. Within less than a decade the religious parties had gone from possessing a majority to being a minor coalition partner. This rapid decline produced an atmosphere conducive to collaboration among the three confessional parties, and after much consultation, a joint list called the Christian Democratic Appeal (CDA) was presented for the 1977 election. This joint list successfully stopped the haemorrhaging of religious electoral support, and the three parties – which had previously begun discussing a possible merger as early as 1968 – received impetus and formally merged before the subsequent election.

The 1977 election was a landslide victory for the PvdA, which gained 10 new seats – an increase of 23 per cent – but their gains were not from where they had hoped they would come. The formation of the CDA had stopped the centre parties' loss of seats to the PvdA. The extreme left parties, on the other hand, were diminished from 16 seats in 1972 to only six in 1977. The gains made by the PvdA thus appear to have come mainly at the expense of the extreme left parties, thereby not increasing the total strength of the left bloc. However, the PvdA still perceived the 1977 results as a victory and entered the coalition negotiations with stringent demands. These demands included the following: (1) the position of Prime Minister; (2) the cabinet should be a progressive one with a PvdA majority of ministers; and (3) binding agreements should be concluded on issues of symbolic significance, such as the extension of the power of workers' councils in the running of industry and the allocation of profits to a national fund mainly controlled by union representatives.

The 1977 election brought gains not only to the PvdA and CDA, but to the VVD as well. A majority coalition could now be formed between the CDA and the VVD. Due to the impossible demands made by the PvdA during its negotiations with the CDA, the latter began to explore the possibility of forming a coalition with the VVD. A cabinet programme was agreed on within days, and a religious–liberal government was installed – 207 days after the election had taken place! The PvdA had won the election but lost the government. Daalder summarized the situation succinctly:

> The deliberate mutual polarization between the Socialist and the Liberals (as the alternative poles on the Left and the Right of the political spectrum) helped these parties to collect votes, which had once been dispersed among the smaller Left and Right parties. (Daalder, 1979: 190)

These findings are supported by Dittrich (1987: 224–8), who analysed the manifestos of the Dutch parties during the post-war period and assessed how their positions moved over the years along the left–right continuum. Dittrich generated a scale and showed that the PvdA fluctuated back and forth across approximately 10 per cent of the scale between 1946 and the late 1960s, with the VVD making similar moves about 20 per cent of the scale to the right of the PvdA. But, in the late 1960s, the PvdA broke sharply to the left, moving twice the distance it had moved for the first 20 years. This was followed by a sharp break to the right by the VVD, creating a gap between the moderate left and moderate right covering almost one-half the range of the entire scale – thereby more than doubling the usual distance between them. The religious parties, throughout almost the entire period, were located in the middle between the two shifting categories. Survey data based on the issue positions of parliament members corroborated these findings and showed that by the late 1970s the PvdA and the VVD placed themselves furthest apart on practically all issues (Daalder, 1987: 207–8).

Realizing that their gains were not from the centre, and that both liberals and the religious parties had registered gains as well, the PvdA came to the conclusion that the polarization strategy it had adopted three elections previously had backfired. The reasons for the polarizing strategy's failure were as follows: (1) the left bloc was nowhere near a parliamentary majority; (2) the right bloc had expanded its share of the seats by a larger ratio; and (3) the religious centre bloc had successfully confronted the polarization and managed not only to hold onto both its pivotal position and central location, but to consolidate and augment its electoral support.

In short, the polarization strategy aimed at splitting or destroying the diminishing religious centre helped force it down the road to merger. The centre position of the CDA afforded it the leverage and power which it had thought was lost when the religious parties dropped below a majority. The result was that by 1977 the CDA demanded parity in the number of ministerial positions, and by 1981 it was once again the biggest party in the Tweede Kamer and demanded the prime ministership. In the aftermath of the failed polarization strategy, the PvdA tried to regain the moderate left position it had forsaken a decade earlier. Its stated policy in the 1980s was a coalition with the CDA and possibly D'66, but not with the PPR, PSP or CPN. In the long run the centrifugal forces were defeated and the Dutch parties returned to their centripetal tactics. Daalder stated that there have been *no* lasting centrifugal drives; a deliberate attempt to 'polarize' the party system by setting up opposing coalitions of parties, has come to nought and has ended in all major parties returning to a policy of wooing votes at the center of Dutch politics. (Daalder, 1989: 14, italics in original)

The disappearance of the strategy of polarization became apparent after the refusal of the PvdA to enter even into a tactical electoral alliance for saving extra votes with the extreme left parties prior to the 1986 election. The formation of a socialist–religious coalition after the following election in 1989 led Wolinetz to argue that

it is possible that the 1989 election will have marked the definitive end of the polarization strategy which the Socialists pursued in one form or another from 1969 to the mid-1980s and the resumption of a pattern of center–left cooperation characteristic of the 1950s. (Wolinetz, 1990: 286)

The polarizing tendencies introduced by the moderate parties in The Netherlands did not produce radical parties at both extremes, and nor did they reduce the parliamentary strength of the moderate core, made up of governing-oriented moderate and centre parties. The strategy of polarization was aimed at the centre parties – similar to the strategy adopted in Denmark – and here too it failed to achieve its desired goals. On the contrary, it helped accelerate the consolidation of the centre parties – the best counter-strategy to combat polarization. The Netherlands thus lends support to the second explanation – centrifugal patterns introduced by the moderate parties are present in a country with a large centre – despite its lack of corroboration with the first explanation.

In conclusion, there is ample evidence to validate the expected relationship between the movement of the moderate parties along the left–right ideological scale and the level of systemic polarization, as proposed in the model's second explanation. The reduction of a centre to below majority status appears to have motivated the moderate parties into adopting a polarizing strategy which, much like the Danish case, was subsequently found to be unsuccessful and was abandoned. The contemporary Dutch party system, however, became a conflictual one based on the consequences of polarization, not a consociational one resulting from pillarization. The polarization strategy's lasting impact placed the parties and the party system in a much more unstable and vulnerable position than before.

In both Denmark and The Netherlands the moderate parties

introduced a strategy of polarization aimed at the centre, with the goal of either forcing it to align with one of the two emerging blocs or breaking it apart. In both countries polarization failed to achieve its desired goals. The centre parties' counter-strategy was, however, quite different in each case. In Denmark, the centre produced two strategies to combat polarization. The first involved tactical shifts between the two polarizing blocs, agreeing to negotiate with both poles as long as the extremes were excluded. The second strategy involved the emergence of minority governments, which placed the moderate parties in the precarious situation of relying on the support of the centre in order to avoid an alternative majority. The centre parties did not allow such minority government, as long as it remained moderate, to destabilize the party system or the government. In The Netherlands the decline of the religious parties during the period of deconfessionalization also produced two developments which combated the moderate parties' strategy of polarization. The first was the emergence of additional, non-religious, centre parties. These parties allowed the centre to maintain its overall parliamentary strength. The second development was the merger of the three religious parties into the CDA, which attempted to reduce its confessional dimension, assume several characteristics of a catch-all party, and increase its share of the secular vote. The centre in both countries thus took the necessary steps to stabilize and maintain the centre-based party system, which successfully put an end to the moderate parties' attempts at polarization.

Part IV

Theoretical Implications

Refining the Model

11.1 The Search for a Relationship

The intuitive conceptualization of the centre as a force of moderation pervades much of the literature that deals with party systems, is accepted almost universally by political scientists, and has achieved the status of an axiom when politics are commonly discussed. This research leads to the conclusion that the intuitive conceptualization could, under certain conditions, be a rather dubious one which is incorrect.

The perception of a moderating centre results from the belief that those who vote for a centre party – and the party which represents these voters – are amenable to negotiations with either the right or the left, are open to compromise and are liable to seek a broader consensus on divisive issues. What this approach fails to take into account, despite the unquestionably moderate characteristics possessed by the centre, is the effect that the centre has on the other parties in the system.

If a particular party system possesses a centre party, or parties, whose parliamentary strength is on the rise, which parties lose the seats now won by the centre? If the centre is truly a moderating factor in the party system, it should win seats from parties across the entire political spectrum – a general trend of voter movement towards the centre. In other words, the fringes should lose seats to the right and left poles of the party system, which, in turn, should lose seats to the centre. However, this research points to the possibility of a third, alternative scenario in which the two main poles, right and left, lose seats to both the centre and the extremes. In such a situation an increase in the centre's parliamentary strength is associated with an opposing trend – the rise of the extreme parties – which counters any moderating impact.

Moreover, if a party system possesses centre parties, will the other parties agree to negotiate, compromise and seek a consensus with the centre? Or will these parties be unwilling to let the centre be the pivotal broker of the system? An affirmative response to the first query would mean the creation of a centre-based party system in which both parties and voters converge on the centre. A positive reply to the second would mean the destruction of a centre-based party system through the attempt to neutralize the centre's influence.

The intuitive interpretation of the centre as a moderating factor would lead one to conclude that the centre will become the pivot of consensual coalitions. As the centre gains more parliamentary seats, both the right and the left will be forced to adopt one of two tactics: post-election results will lead them to realize the necessity of centre-based coalitions which mandate compromise; or pre-election manoeuvring to win back voters will lead them to adopt positions closer to the centre. Both tactics will result in a moderation of the party system.

However, this research points to the possibility that the growth of the centre will not produce a moderation of the party system. According to an alternative scenario, the centre's potential coalition partners – the parties on the moderate right and left – pull away in an outward pattern with the goal of creating a two-bloc, bipolar party system. This goal is to be achieved by providing the voters with only two credible alternatives from which to choose, left and right, thereby coercing the centre to either join one of the two sides or be eliminated from the group of possible coalition partners – consequently eradicating its *raison d'être*.

The alternative approaches to the centre stress the immoderate characteristics possessed by centre parties and their possible impacts on the party system – centrifugal competition and enhanced polarization. These seemingly counter-intuitive approaches would lead one to conclude either that there is a connection between the growth of centre and extreme parties, or that the party system will not allow the centre to become pivotal and dominate the process of coalition-making – both bringing on a centrifugal pattern of electoral competition resulting in the polarization of the party system.

Based on the desire to test the intuitive conceptualization of the centre on the one hand, and the opposing alternative perception on the other, the primary hypothesis for this research was formulated: there is a relationship between the parliamentary strength of centre parties and the level of party system polarization. This hypothesis was tested in two stages and was based on the adoption of two criteria. The first criterion used was the location of parties along a 10-point, left–right, unidimensional ideological continuum. The second criterion was the collapsing of this scale into five categories: extreme left and right, moderate left and right, and centre.

The first stage of the test was a statistical analysis of election results from a majority of the European parliamentary systems between 1979 and 1989. This analysis produced no support for the primary hypothesis. There appears to be no relationship between the parliamentary strength of centre parties and the level of systemic polarization. As the parliamentary size of the centre parties varied ten-fold among the various country cases, from 5 per cent to almost 50 per cent of the seats, the level of party system polarization remained quite stable.

Two underlying explanations for the lack of a relationship were then theoretically inferred and empirically corroborated, in the attempt to construct a model which would show that a relationship between centre parties and polarization does indeed exist. The first explanation uncovered two concurrent trends: as we move from those cases with a small centre to those with a large one, the extremist parties' share of parliamentary seats also grew. The second explanation revealed another coinciding pattern: as we moved from small to large centre party cases, the moderate parties pushed away from the centre. In both of the explanations, the latter trend served to offset the moderating impact of the former trend based on the centre parties' growing share of parliamentary seats, and therefore the result was a relatively consistent level of party system polarization. Both explanations in the model are contrary to the moderating conceptualization of the centre.

The second phase of testing involved two in-depth case studies, in order to assess which of the two explanations in the model was more conclusive. These case studies revealed a negation of the first explanation – extremist parties gaining seats alongside the centre parties – and an affirmation of the second explanation – an outward movement of the moderate parties. That is, as we move from a small to a large centre, the centre's share of parliamentary seats is related both positively and negatively to the level of systemic polarization: positively due to the rise in the parliamentary strength of the centre; negatively due to the growing distance between the two moderate poles of the system.

11.2 Analysis and Generalizations

The lack of a relationship between the centre parties' share of parliamentary seats and the level of party system polarization is not due to a mistaken intuitive perception of the centre, but rather to an inadequate one. As we move from those cases with a small centre to those with a large one the party system is indeed moderated, but a synchronic attempt to polarize the system appears as well. A more adequate perception of the centre should, therefore, take both trends into account. Generalizing from this model leads to the conclusion that an increase in the centre's share of parliamentary seats can produce two contrasting systemic processes, moderation and polarization – in other words, centripetal and centrifugal patterns of electoral competition.

The first explanation in the model posits that there is a positive relationship between centre and extreme parties' share of parliamentary seats only when the centre is large. In the case of a small centre – defined as up to 20 per cent of the parliamentary seats – no relationship existed. In the two case studies, Denmark represented the small centre and The Netherlands the large centre countries. The Dutch case, therefore, should have empirically validated the first explanation – but it surprisingly produced the opposite conclusion. That is, while the Danish case showed no relationship where none was expected, the Dutch case showed no relationship where one was assumed to exist. The first explanation was, therefore, confirmed on its weakest and least substantial aspects, but rejected when its strongest and most significant findings were analysed.

The model's second explanation argues that the moderate parties on both the right and the left push away from the centre as we move from the small to the large centre cases. If either the Danish or the Dutch case verified this relationship, then the second explanation could be considered significant. Its significance would, however, be enhanced if both cases substantiated the outward movement of parties. Moreover, this explanation and its contribution to party systems theory would attain its full weight only if both cases supported its findings and if a stronger centrifugal movement could be shown to occur in the Dutch case – the large centre country – than in the Danish case. The reason for this is that not only could the movement from small to large centre cases be related to a process of polarization, but such movement would also be positively correlated with polarization – exhibiting an exacerbated polarizing trend in the large centre case. The analysis of the Danish and Dutch case studies did provide empirical validation for the most stringent requirements – centrifugal trends were found in both, and they were more acute in the Dutch case.

The stronger centrifugal trend exhibited in the large centre case study is substantiated by referring to a simple differentiation in party behaviour: pre-election electoral strategies versus post-election parliamentary tactics. The Danish case showed that the moderate parties moved away from the centre. However, this centrifugal process began only after the 1966 election gave the moderate left Social Democrats (SD) and the extreme left Socialist People's Party (SF) a workers' majority for the first time. There were no attempts by the SD to court its extremist fringe prior to the election. On the contrary, the extreme left had become accustomed to the cold-shoulder policy of the moderate left. When these parties did indeed begin to co-operate, the extremist SF never became a full coalition partner. It simply provided parliamentary support for a minority SD government. Only when the voters provided these parties with a majority in parliament, and thereby a credible opportunity to transform the tripolar and centre-based party system into a two-bloc system, did they adopt a strategy of polarization. When the electorate ceased to provide results that were conducive to two-bloc politics, the polarization tactics were abandoned by the parties.

The Dutch case, on the other hand, also showed the moderate parties moving away from the centre, but this was a predetermined and deliberate pre-election tactic aimed at providing the voters with a clear two-bloc choice of party alliances. When Labour (PvdA), Democrats '66 (D'66) and the Radicals (PPR) presented a joint programme and a co-ordinated slate of ministers to the voters prior to the 1971 and 1972 elections, these parties were far from the threshold of a parliamentary majority.[1] The polarization strategy in The Netherlands was not the consequence of specific election results, but was adopted in order to cause a particular electoral outcome. The moderate left actively courted the parties on the extreme left before the elections, and had the stated goal of pushing the centre to ally with either the left or the right – a bipolar system. The coalition formed after the 1972 election included a party that was quickly becoming extremist in nature, the PPR, and which remained part of the government well past the point when it crossed into the extreme left camp. In other words, the Dutch case demonstrates not only a deliberate pre-election strategy, it also embraced extremist elements more willingly than the Danish case. Only when the centre refused to align with one of the two emerging blocs, and decided to confront the polarization head-on by merging the three religious parties into a seemingly catch-all centre party, was polarization forsaken. Therefore, the strategy of polarization was enacted due to systemic reasons and goals, but was manifested by electoral tactics. It was abandoned because of the same systemic considerations, regardless of the electoral gains it had accumulated for both the moderate right and the moderate left in the short term. This process is almost the inverse of the Danish case.

Therefore, in both case studies the outward movement of the moderate parties – not the simultaneous increase in both centre and extreme party seats – served to undermine the moderating influence of the centre. The result was the rather constant level of party system polarization. Moreover, the polarization strategy was found to be more aggressive in the case study with a large centre. That is, in order to maintain the level of systemic polarization, the centrifugal movement of the moderate parties was stronger in the case where the centre held a larger share of parliamentary seats. An attempt to generalize from the two case studies would lead to the assertion that in those countries where the centre parties are already sizeable, and are increasing their share of parliamentary seats, the moderate parties' attempt to polarize the party system will become more apparent and aggravated.

In short, the reason for the rather constant level of party system polarization, despite a continued increase in the share of centre party seats, is the outward movement of the moderate parties – a 'moderate-induced' strategy of polarization. This centrifugal pattern is evident even in those countries with a small centre, and becomes magnified in those countries with a large centre.

11.3   The Performance of the Centre

The Danish and Dutch cases demonstrate a similar scenario in which the centre parties become the target of polarization initiated by the moderate parties, specifically the moderate left. In the first case, the centre was small, and the turbulent changes in Danish politics and society opened it up to a frontal attack from its surrounding parties. In the second case, the centre was large, but volatile shifts in Dutch politics and society eroded its parliamentary strength and thereby exposed it to a similar assault.

The centres in both countries enjoyed a level of political influence far beyond their relative size, especially the Danish centre. There are two main reasons for this: position and performance. Position refers to the location of the centre parties between two opposing ideological blocs, neither of which was able to gain a parliamentary majority. Performance refers to the ability of the centre parties to negotiate with both blocs, and to form the pivot of alternating coalitions with either. That is, the centres in both countries were also in the middles of their respective party systems. However, the exaggerated level of political influence attained by the centre also made it a target for attack.

Whereas the centre parties were content to continue their pivotal role for the foreseeable future, neither of the major blocs to the right and left appeared willing to allow this. The moderate right and moderate left were forced to play by the centre's rules, and were coerced into giving up some of their political leverage in order to form a government with the centre. The dream of both moderate camps, though, was to govern alone. Their inability to pursue and enact their interests, and the constant concessions made to the centre, brought about enhanced competition from the extremes. The extremes capitalized on the inability of either moderate pole to push through its agenda, and on the exaggerated influence awarded to the centre. However, this study has not found any relationship between the parliamentary strength of centre parties and that of the extreme parties. The growth of the extreme parties, if such a trend is present, is not related to the centre.

The moderate parties, much like the centre parties, found themselves squeezed from both sides. Their only choice became the direction of competition – would they move centripetally in order to attract centre voters, or centrifugally in order to capture the more radical ones? Since there were more voters in the centre than at the extremes, the intuitive choice would have been a centripetal strategy. However, much as with the inadequate intuitive moderating perception of the centre, the empirical evidence proves otherwise. The decision, in both cases, was the latter – a centrifugal movement away from the centre.

There is a good reason for this choice by the moderate parties to introduce a strategy of polarization. Had the moderate parties adopted a centripetal pattern, they might have lost more voters than they would have gained. The centre parties, despite their voter volatility, appear to be quite stable in the long term. In other words, the part of the electorate located between the left and right poles – the traditional floating vote – is, by and large, either a loyal centre electorate or one that cannot bring itself to switch to the opposite pole, and thus becomes identified with, or at least supportive of, the centre. This means that the centrally located voters cannot be easily captured by a minor movement of the moderate parties towards the centre; they must be courted and won over by a serious and meaningful centripetal electoral strategy. But this would only have exacerbated the cause of the extreme parties, and some moderate voters would have most likely defected to them. Therefore, a convincing move towards the centre by the moderate parties could have possibly gained more voters than it would have lost, but there is no assurance of this, and the outcome could just as easily have been the opposite.

A centrifugal strategy, on the other hand, appeared to be more appealing. The moderate parties could regain the voters they had lost to the extremes, while simultaneously avoiding a loss of votes to the centre. The latter was accomplished by offering the voters two clear-cut choices: left or right. Centre-based coalitions would no longer be tolerated, so the polarizing electoral strategy implied, and voting for the centre was therefore counter-productive. Any socialist who voted for the centre made it less likely that the socialists would gain power, and more likely that the conservatives would do so because the centre would agree to a coalition with the right. The conservatives used similar appeals against the centre. Co-operation between the moderate and extreme parties on each side, respectively, made the anti-centre tactic that much more credible, and appeared to single out the centre as the only category not under consideration for inclusion in the next government. Both the centre and the floating voters were then faced with a dilemma: should they vote once more for the centre which had always played a role in government, or would such a vote become either ineffectual this time, or even allow the less favoured of the two camps to gain power alone?

The centre found itself caught between two poles who no longer sought to co-operate with it – the moderate-induced strategy of polarization – but it still sought to base its appeal on its continued ability to co-operate with both. Moreover, the centre had traditionally refused to associate with the extremes, which further hindered its continued possession of the broker role during the period of moderate–extreme collaboration. The centre thus presented itself as the defender of the old system – the centre-based, moderate and consensual party system. It promised to continue its policies of negotiating with either bloc, and of not joining any government based on the support of extreme parties. At this stage the existence of a centre and the performance of the centre became two opposing and, as this research has shown, offsetting patterns. The existence of a centre in a party system with a majority neither to its left nor to its right – the definition of a pivotal centre party – elicited a pattern of moderate-induced polarizing competition meant to force the centre into one of the two poles, or to eradicate it. The performance of the centre, on the other hand, has always been that of a moderating factor, and during the strategy of polarization this became the *sine qua non* of its tactics and appeals for centripetal, moderating competition.

In Denmark, the centre parties have had a considerable inflow and outflow of voters, but have surprisingly kept their relative stability in overall support. The biggest centre party, the Radical Liberals (RV), had the most unfaithful voters, matched by only one other party, the Centre Democrats (CD) – also a centre party. Nonetheless, the RV led the other centre parties in the adoption and execution of an historical moderating role. The RV had, until recently, participated only in majority coalitions and had been part of every majority coalition in post-war Denmark. The party entered its first minority coalition only in 1988 – 20 years after the last majority coalition was formed in Denmark – even though the minority status of most Danish governments had usually depended on the centre for its survival. Some centre parties formally became part of a coalition, but others served as brokers in parliament to help form majorities, either to the right or to the left, in order to pass most policies. The CD and the Christian People's Party (KRF), two parties which emerged out of protest against both left and right, turned out to follow the RV and play the role of true centre parties. Bille stated that

> although born in protest, their actual performance in the Folketing demonstrated that they were pragmatic parties which were willing to compromise on nearly every issue. Thus, for example, along with the Social–Liberal Party [RV], which had refused to support a government which was dependent on the support of an extreme party, they took a clear stand against extremist tendencies, constantly emphasizing the need to reach agreements 'across the center'. For these parties, it became an ideology and a *raison d'être* to compromise and to mediate. (Bille, 1989: 53)

The Danish centre thus became a core of parties which: (1) possessed the ability to manoeuvre between alliances with the moderate right or the moderate left; (2) took a united stand against any participation by the extreme parties; and (3) participated in most policy formation processes as the provider of the majority. The moderate-induced strategy of polarization was aimed at destroying this role that the centre core played, but it did not succeed. The failure is partly due to the centre parties' ability to correctly oppose this strategy. At first, the centre allied with the moderate right in order to oppose the moderate left governing with the extreme left. When a minority-led SD government was formed, with the support of the extremist SF, the Danish party system was on the verge of bipolarity. The centre parties, in response, allied themselves with the bourgeois parties in the attempt to oppose and undermine the co-operation between the moderate and extreme left. However, as soon as the left bloc fell below a majority, the centre detached itself from the moderate right and once again adopted a central position, agreeing to negotiate with both poles as long as the extremes were excluded.

The minority status of Danish governments since 1971 has placed them in a precarious situation – if they did not gain the support of the centre parties they would face an 'alternative majority' in the Folketing. But the centre parties took strong steps in the attempt to stabilize their centre-based party system. The manifestation of just such an 'alternative majority' would have brought down governments in the past, but, more recently, the government has remained in power even if defeated on a variety of issues. The centre parties have thus sought to weaken governments, but not to destroy them. As long as the minority government co-operated with the centre, it was not forced to accept alternative policies passed by the majority in opposition. This strategy allowed the centre to: (1) maximize its political influence; (2) achieve a renewed level of moderation in the party system; and (3) maintain stability despite the minority status and weak nature of the government. In short, it was the tactics, actions and performance of the centre parties themselves which played a crucial role in halting the moderate-induced polarizing drive towards a two-bloc party system in Denmark, and in the re-emergence of a multipolar, moderate system.

The Dutch case is quite similar. The decline of the religious parties during the period of deconfessionalization revealed a growing number of floating voters who had left the religious fold and could be attracted by any party. The socialist PvdA, and subsequently the Liberals (VVD), decided not only to attract these voters but to seek additional ones as well, by exacerbating the demise of the religious parties. The strategy adopted here was also one of moderate-induced centrifugal competition aimed at creating a bipolar party system. However, two developments helped raise obstacles to this strategy that soon made it fail.

The first development was the emergence of additional non-religious centre parties. These parties made it possible for the traditional religious voter to avoid choosing between remaining a religious voter and becoming an anti-religious one. That is, the new minor centre parties allowed the previously confessional voters to switch parties without immediately supporting those parties that carried a tradition of animosity towards their former affiliation. Moreover, these minor parties quickly adopted a centre position and functioned much like the religious parties in their advocacy of centre-based coalitions. Indeed, there is no direct relationship between the decline of the religious parties and the rise of the PvdA and VVD, while the best gains of the secular parties

– in the 1977 election – came at the point when the confessional losses
had been successfully halted. Therefore, the shift of previously confessional supporters to the new minor centre parties allowed the centre to
maintain its overall parliamentary strength.

The second development was the merger of the three religious
parties into the Christian Democratic Appeal (CDA), which eventually
took on the characteristics of a catch-all centre party. The CDA began to
attract voters based on issues, rather than on religion, and increased its
share of the secular vote. This merger, therefore, brought about the
creation of a strong centre party that could not be split between the
right and left blocs, and it produced a moderate point of attraction at
the centre of the party system for both confessional and secular voters.
The strategy of polarization was aimed at a declining religious centre
which could only compete 'defensively' to maintain its voter base. In
response to this strategy, the dwindling religious centre was replaced by
a growing secular centre which was now able to undertake 'expansive'
competition in the search for new voters. Daalder pointed out that

> a centre rapidly losing its traditional voting support, potentially replacing
> it by a plebiscitary appeal, is an ironic outcome of the process of change
> ... in which the left tried to introduce the principle of alternative
> government in a system where it did not command enough votes to make
> a success of its policy of 'democratic' polarization. (Daalder, 1986: 530)

The centre parties in The Netherlands, much like those in Denmark,
are thus partially responsible for the emergence of moderate-induced
polarization aimed at bringing about a bipolar system, but their response and performance are mostly responsible for its termination and
the return to moderate pluralist politics.

Through (1) the creation of new parties and (2) the merger and
adaptation of older ones, the centre once again came to possess the
dominant party in the Dutch party system and also became the predominant category, resting on just below one-half of the parliamentary
seats. However, it did not regain its lost majority.

The empirical manifestations concerning the performance of the
centre are thus present in both of the case studies. Similar findings were
uncovered in a third case, based on a study of the centre in Chile by
Scully (1992). Scully divided the history of the Chilean party system in
the nineteenth and twentieth centuries into three phases, and illustrated how the performance of the centre helped stabilize the party
system during the first two, but then destabilized it in the third.[2] During
the first two phases, the centre parties in Chile acted in a manner akin

to that of the Danish and Dutch centres, and they had a corresponding impact on the party system. During the first phase Scully wrote that

> without the continued existence of the centre, political competition would have been more, not less, polarized … The moderating role played by parties of the center … allowed a pattern of interaction between parties to emerge which favored political accommodation. (Scully, 1992: 57)

The second phase produced a similar conclusion concerning the centre parties' contribution (Scully, 1992: 103): 'their moderating presence at the center of the party system contributed to the basically centripetal direction of political competition and facilitated the transition to competitive party politics'. However, during the third phase the centre ceased to perform in accordance with its previous nature, and began to push for fundamental and uncompromising principles to which it became committed. As Scully (1992: 183) stated, the centre 'rejected the policies of both the right and the left and offered a third fundamental alternative, a "third pole" within the party system'. This shift in the centre's nature helped bring about heightened polarization and led to the breakdown of party politics in 1973.

Scully thus places the burden of exacerbated polarization on the performance and nature of the centre, whereas this study places it on the mere presence of a centre – particularly a large, precarious and pivotal one. According to Scully's analysis, there are two different types of centre parties: positional and programmatic:

> A positional center party is one that takes an intermediate, compromising position with respect to the extreme poles along the predominant axis of political conflict … In contrast, a programmatic center party is substantially committed to a specific set of policies and a particular outcome along the principal axis of cleavage on which it is unwilling or unable to compromise. (Scully, 1992: 11)

The core of this difference is that positional centre parties are incidental to the primary cleavage of conflict, thereby allowing them the freedom to manoeuvre between right and left and to act as brokers, as opposed to programmatic centre parties, which are fundamental to the predominant cleavage and cannot compromise with both sides, thereby losing the mediating role (Scully, 1992: 180–6).

Scully did, however, point to the centrifugal movement of the surrounding parties – the focus of this study's findings – which coincided with the growth of the centre. For example, in the late 1950s and early 1960s the centre-right Radical Party moved rightwards, closer to the moderate right Conservative Party, to form the Democratic Front; meanwhile, the moderate and extreme left parties (Socialists and Marxists) within the FRAP coalition moved further leftwards; at the same time the share of the vote won by the centrist Christian Democrats rose from 9.4 per cent in 1957 to 22.8 per cent in 1963. The centrifugal trend continued throughout the 1960s. Scully pointed out that

> Christian Democratic policies of agrarian reform and peasant union-ization, increased property taxes and modified property rights pushed the right further to the right and led to deeper alienation from the center ... Christian Democratic reforms were so far-reaching that the left – already undergoing a process of radicalization – was pushed even further leftward. (Scully, 1992: 163, 166)

This study shows that polarization was initiated in both the Danish and Dutch party systems without the centre changing its nature and per-formance. That is, regardless of the centre's nature – positional or programmatic – its mere existence can elicit a polarizing trend. More-over, in agreement with Scully's findings, if the centre parties abandon their pattern of co-operation with the moderate parties, this can serve as an additional element in pushing the moderate parties to adopt a centrifugal strategy of electoral competition. Nonetheless, the presence of a centre, especially a vulnerable and sizeable one, is the necessary factor.

Notes

[1.] It is true that the centrist D'66 joined the progressive alliance prior to the 1971 and 1972 elections, which included the PvdA and PPR, but it was due to the objections of D'66 that the extremist Communist (CPN) and Pacifist Socialist (PSP) parties were not included in the alliance. Moreover, at the time the PPR was still considered by most to belong to the moderate left, and only since 1977 has the party become part of the extreme left.

[2.] One should note that the expansive historical analysis presented by Scully covers periods in which the centre was constituted by different parties. During the first period of his analysis the centre was made up of the Liberals, located between the Radicals and Conservatives; in the second period it was the Radicals, located between the Communists and Socialists on the one side and the Conservatives and Liberals on the other; in the third period it was the Christian Democrats, located between the Communists and Socialists on the one side (later Popular Unity) and the Radicals, Conservatives and Liberals on the other (later the Democratic Front, followed by the Nationals).

12

Applications for Party Systems, Electoral Competition and Government Stability

12.1   Centre Parties and Centre Tendencies

At the outset of this study, when the paradox of the centre was presented, two questions were raised. Does the centre disintegrate in the face of escalating competition over opposing fundamental principles? Or, in order to survive, does it set a trend in motion that allows it to capitalize on enhanced divisiveness? This study's findings lead to the conclusion that the answer to the first question is negative, whereas the answer to the second is positive.

In both of the case studies analysed, the centre did not disintegrate when faced with polarizing competition. However, when competition escalated, the centre presented itself as the alternative to the extreme parties in the formation of a future government with the moderate parties, and was able not only to maintain its share of seats but even to increase it. Thus, the centre did capitalize on enhanced divisiveness. What these questions do not take into account is that the centre was also responsible, in part, for the emergence of moderate-induced polarizing electoral competition. The mere existence of centre parties, especially when they are vulnerable and occupy a pivotal position in a reasonably balanced party system, is a stimulus for polarization. In other words, using the terminology proposed in this study, when centre parties are simultaneously middle parties the centre can be a cause of polarized electoral competition.

These findings are particularly germane to the theoretical debate on the centre between Duverger and Sartori, and they appear to settle their argument. In accordance with the findings, Duverger's (1959: 215) statement that 'there may well be a Centre party but there is no centre tendency, no centre doctrine' is apparently wrong. This research has shown that there is such a thing as a centre tendency, i.e. the prevalence of centripetal competition supported by the implementation of what this study defines as a centre doctrine (see Section 12.2). This centre doctrine is the stimulus for the emergence of a strategy of polarization by the moderate parties – as opposed to the more intuitive strategy that these parties might have adopted. Moreover, a centre tendency is also the tactic used to undermine the moderate-induced strategy of polarization aimed at the centre.

Furthermore, despite the support the findings have given to Sartori's theoretical framework, his reversal of Duverger's statement, 'a center opinion, or a center tendency, always exists in politics; what may not exist is a center party' (Sartori, 1966: 156), remains questionable. Sartori perceived a negative association between centre parties and centre tendencies. 'The very existence of a center party (or parties) discourages "centrality"' (Sartori, 1976: 135). That is, a party system is characterized by a centre tendency only when the centre is vacant – when the moderate and centrally located electorate does not have a party to identify with. This study's findings show that it is not necessarily an either/or phenomenon. A party system with a centre party can still exhibit a centre tendency. The party system does not require a vacant centre in order to be characterized by a centre tendency. A centre tendency does not necessitate a centrally located, unidentified, floating electorate and a vacant centre. Moreover, a strong centre party with identified voters does not necessarily offset a convergence towards the centre. In short, the very existence of a strong centre party, notwithstanding its impact on increased systemic polarization, does not discourage 'centrality'. Centre parties can, and do, exist while simultaneously cultivating a centre tendency.

On the other hand, the findings do support Sartori's claim that a centrifugal push can be started at the centre. That is, there does exist a relationship between the centre parties' share of seats and the outward movement of the moderate parties. While the existence of a centre party, or parties, does not discourage centripetal competition, it is conducive to the introduction of centrifugal competition based on an outward movement of parties. The growth of the centre thus exhibits two contrasting characteristics: it enhances centripetal competition, thereby moderating the party system, and it inaugurates centrifugal competition, thereby polarizing the party system. It is these two opposing patterns that keep the level of party system polarization reasonably stable as the centre parties increase their share of parliamentary seats ten-fold.

12.2 A Centre Doctrine

Contrary to Sartori's framework, the physical occupation of the centre does not necessarily imply that the moderate electorate is no longer the floating electorate – the Danish centre parties, for example, are characterized by volatility and disloyalty. But, in agreement with Sartori, the parties surrounding the centre perceived the centre voters to be loyal enough that it swayed their decision over which tactics to pursue – centripetal versus centrifugal competition – in the direction of polarization. The moderate parties in both Denmark and The Netherlands did not believe that a movement towards the centre could win over a significant amount of voters, but the centre still remained the target of their attack. Their resulting mobilization strategy was not to converge on the centre, but to move away from it and force it either to join one side or to be torn apart.

Thus, it was the existence of centre parties in Denmark and The Netherlands which dissuaded and diverted the initial centripetal tactics of the moderate parties, in exchange for centrifugal tactics based on collaboration with more extremist elements. The response of the centre parties in both countries – continued advocacy of centre-based coalitions and opposition to any government relying on extremist parties – showed that, contrary to Duverger (1959: 215), the centre is not 'an artificial grouping of the right wing of the Left and the left wing of the Right'. Had this assumption been true, the polarization strategy in both countries should have succeeded in tearing apart the centre.

Furthermore, the amalgamation and merger of the Dutch religious parties into a secular mass party, based on the strategy of maintaining a central orientation for both the party system and any future coalition, showed the underlying characteristic of what may be called a 'centre doctrine' which helped lead towards the re-emergence of a centre tendency. Based on this study's findings, it is now possible to begin to define what a centre doctrine is, and to posit that it can be responsible for the emergence of two opposing trends: polarization and a centre tendency. The preliminary definition of a centre doctrine is: (1) the ability to negotiate with both the moderate right and the moderate left; (2) the refusal to join any government relying on extremist support; (3) the desire to emphasize agreements 'across the centre'; and (4) the continuous advocacy of the need for compromise, moderation and consensual politics. It was the pursuit of a centre doctrine by the centre parties which helped counter the moderate-induced strategies of polarization and returned both the Dutch and Danish party systems to a centre tendency.

The existence of a centre thus concurrently discourages and encourages centripetal competition, contrary to Sartori's framework. More precisely, the presence of parties at the centre discourages other parties from adopting a centripetal strategy to gain new voters, but the centre parties continue using counter-polarization strategies to appeal to the moderate electorate in the attempt to encourage a return to the pattern of centripetal competition. The centre could lose in either case. If polarization is successful, then the centre will either break apart or join one of the opposing blocs. If, on the other hand, moderate electoral competition successfully returns, then centre voters might be lost to the now converging moderate parties. The success of polarization would, therefore, destroy the centre parties and any possibility for a centre tendency. The success of moderation, however, could cripple the centre parties, but a centre tendency would survive.

Once again, the conclusion is that a centre tendency can exist with or without centre parties. While the presence of centre parties can serve as the accelerator for underlying polarization, it could then also become the saviour of a moderate systemic constellation. Therefore, in agreement with Sartori, a centre positioning of parties is a cause of polarization; but it is also a force of moderation. This outcome is consistent with Scully's conclusion concerning the centre's impact on the Chilean party system, where he stated that

> Sartori's injunction that 'the very existence of a center party (or parties) discourages "centrality", i.e. the centripetal drives of the political system' notwithstanding, the centripetal drive underlying the Chilean party system has been enhanced in decisive ways by the presence and behavior of a major party at the center. (Scully, 1992: 199)

Both in Denmark, where the centre is small, and in The Netherlands, where the centre is large, polarization was the strategy adopted by the moderate parties in order to attack the centre and win over the centre voters. Even in the case of Denmark, the small centre was able to alter the competitive configuration of the party system at least twice – once as the stimulus for the adoption of moderate-induced polarization, and once as the force behind the return to moderation. In The Netherlands the impact of the centre was similar, with two caveats: first, the strategy of polarization was adopted only when the centre fell below majority status; second, polarization was more extensive than in Denmark. This leads to the reaffirmation of the previous conclusion that as the parliamentary strength of the centre parties rises, the strategy of polarization adopted by the moderate parties will be more acute and divisive. However, when the centre is beyond the threshold of a majority the moderate parties perceive it to be too strong and stable, and do not attempt to polarize the party system.

Polarization can, therefore, be related to the centre. However, it appears that the existence of stable centre parties is not sufficient to produce polarization. As long as the centre parties in Denmark and The Netherlands were part of a stable and structured party system, there was little or no polarization. Only when instability was introduced into the party system, as a result of socio-economic transformations in the polity which produced enhanced electoral volatility, did polarization manifest itself. That is, only when the centre no longer appeared to be impenetrable did the moderate parties attempt to attack it by polarizing the system. The larger the centre parties are at the moment of vulnerability, the harsher the strategy of polarization. But, if the centre is able to hold onto its pivotal position, while performing in accordance with a centre doctrine, it can successfully counter the polarization attempt. As both Denmark and The Netherlands show, the moderate parties did not achieve their goal of a majority and abandoned their centrifugal strategies, reversing their movement back towards the centre. Yet, as the two case studies also show, the moderate parties did not go all the way back to their original positions, and the party systems ended up in a more polarized state than they were in prior to the advent of polarization.

In summary, Sartori's analysis of the centre is more valid than that of Duverger, despite some disagreements with Sartori's framework which are produced by this research's findings.

12.3   The Centre and Government Stability

The introductory chapter of this study ended with an analysis of how the centre could impact on government stability. The issue can now be stated in a clear manner. The existence of centre parties, particularly vulnerable ones, is conducive to polarization, and polarization enhances the chances for extremist parties to be created and to prosper. Empirical evidence has shown that it is the existence of such extremist parties which impacts negatively on coalition formation and governmental stability. However, this research has shown that there is no evidence to support a positive relationship between centre and extreme parties. Based on empirical evidence from the two case studies, despite the finding that vulnerable centre parties are conducive to polarization, one cannot conclude that the centre is directly associated with the growth or emergence of anti-system or extremist parties.

This research does, however, show that there is ample evidence to support a positive relationship between the centre and a centrifugal movement of the moderate parties. However, the important difference here is that democracy is not threatened. The moderate parties, tired of having to constantly rely on the centre in order to form a governing coalition, adopt a strategy of polarization in order to force the centre voters to choose between right and left. It is true that co-operation with extremist parties is part of the strategy, but they are relegated to the role of junior partners and their parliamentary strength does not increase. The goal here is to switch from a tripolar to a bipolar party system. In other words, the moderate parties want to destroy the centre's disproportionate influence, but they do not want to destroy centrism. The moderate parties want to function in a bipolar party constellation similar to that of Britain and France, rather than in the multipolar configurations of Denmark and The Netherlands. Through electoral tactics they seek to attain a type of party system which other countries have achieved by electoral laws. Moderate-induced polarization, therefore, must still be perceived as part of the natural mechanics, drastic as they may seem, of democratic multiparty competition. The success of such a strategy could democratically alter the framework of the party system, but its corollary ramifications are not the destruction of a centre tendency, increased governmental instability and the possible collapse of democracy.

In both Denmark and The Netherlands, the centre was not the instigator of polarization, but was a stimulus for its appearance. If blame needs to be placed, then it should be on the moderate parties who actually caused the rise in systemic polarization. The centre was responsible for the failure of polarization, and the return to a centripetal, moderate and consensual pattern of electoral competition. However, the centre cannot escape the partial responsibility for the increase in systemic polarization. It is an indirect responsibility, with the moderate parties serving as intervening variables – without which any remaining relationship between the centre and polarization has been shown to be spurious. The existence of a centre served as a safety mechanism, almost an insurance policy, against the triumph of polarization. Scully's findings on Chile support this conclusion:

An exploration of more than twelve decades of political competition in Chile indicates that a center may be necessary to act as a broker ... to hold the party system together. The center can act as a mediator ... absorbing potential shocks to the system emanating from the poles. (Scully, 1992: 9)

In short, the potential for polarization might be a constant presence in all party systems. The case studies lead to the conclusion that polarization is manifested by the moderate parties, which are stimulated by the centre parties; but the actions, adaptive capacities and performance of the centre parties prevent the permanent transformation of the party system into a polarized and unstable configuration, returning the party system to a less polarized, but also less moderate, constellation. The result is continued government stability, based on coalitions across the centre. As long as centre parties adhere to a centre doctrine, a centre-based party system can overcome moderate-induced polarization, continue to exhibit a centre tendency and maintain government stability.

12.4   Conclusion

Although there is no *direct* relationship between the parliamentary strength of centre parties and the level of party system polarization, this study has produced several significant findings based on an *indirect* relationship. Generalizing from the cross-national statistical analysis, and the two in-depth case studies, the important patterns which have been uncovered are the following:

1.   The presence, and growth, of centre parties directly impacts on the moderate parties, not the extremist parties.
2.   The moderate parties react by instigating a strategy of electoral and/or systemic polarization.
3.   This polarization is the byproduct of the moderate parties' choice of centrifugal over centripetal tactics to attack the centre.
4.   Moderate-induced polarization does not generate those systemic propensities which are dangerous to government stability.
5.   The centre parties can successfully combat and overcome this moderate-induced polarization strategy.

In both case studies – after the centre lost its majority in The Netherlands – the centre parties had disproportionate power because they were the providers of a majority to either of the two major poles of competition, the left or the right. They were thus simultaneously pivotal centre and pivotal middle parties. This constellation placed both moderate camps, to the right and to the left of the centre, in a situation where neither was able to achieve a parliamentary majority on its own, despite its desire to govern alone. In other words, the centre parties functioned as the king-makers of the Danish and Dutch party systems. The result was that the centre directly influenced the electoral tactics of those parties which surrounded it – the moderate parties who decided to attack the centre, not the extreme parties.

The decision taken by the moderate parties, in both cases, in order to achieve a majority was to transform the tripolar party system into a bipolar one. A bipolar party system *ipso facto* means that either the left or the right will possess a majority. The centre, according to the bipolar strategy, would be forced to ally with one of the two sides – to cease being both centre and middle – or would be torn apart if it refused to do so. Thus far the two cases do not point to any unexpected developments. However, the decision of which strategy to adopt in order to bring about a bipolar system is surprising. Contrary to strategic calculations based on the Downsian model (Downs, 1957) – in which a normal distribution of voters should bring about a convergence of the right and the left in order to win over the centre's supporters – the moderate parties decided to move in the opposite direction, and adopted a strategy of polarizing the party system.

It appears that the moderate parties perceived that the centre's supporters could not be easily converted, despite the volatile nature of these voters. Moreover, any movement towards the centre would alienate moderate supporters, who might switch to the extreme parties. The decision was thus made to adopt centrifugal electoral tactics and move away from the centre. This centrifugal pattern was aimed at giving both centre voters and centre politicians a clear-cut choice between alignment with one of the two camps, or the maintenance of a centre position that would be ineffectual politically in the short term, and would lose support in the long term. In short, the moderate parties decided to destroy the centre's power and, if need be, to destroy the centre as well.

The centre, therefore, has an indirect relationship with polarization. There are, however, certain conditions for the centre's impact: (1) the centre parties should be in a pivotal position; (2) the centre parties should concurrently be the middle parties; (3) the centre's voters should not be perceived as the 'floating vote', which can be easily won over by the other parties; and (4) the moderate parties should seek to govern alone by gaining a parliamentary majority. If these conditions are present, then the moderate parties are likely to adopt electoral tactics that polarize the party system—allying themselves with the extreme parties—in the attempt to attack the centre, destroy its influence and bring about a bipolar party configuration.

An additional finding exposed by this research is that if the centre does not surrender to the moderate-induced strategy of polarization, and adopts what can be termed a centre doctrine, it can then serve as the best possible defence against this strategy. By maintaining its pivotal position and presenting itself to the voters as the only temperate, consensus-oriented parties remaining, the centre is ultimately able to thwart the centrifugal tactics of the moderate parties and maintain the prevalence of centripetal competition—or a centre tendency.

This study began by presenting a paradox. The empirical evidence uncovered proves that the impact of the centre is indeed a paradox: the existence of centre parties serves as the stimulus for the moderate parties to adopt an electoral strategy of polarizing the party system; but, if the centre parties become the champions of moderating electoral competition, they can effectively combat and overcome this polarization.

Appendix

All the parties incorporated in the cross-national statistical analysis are listed below, along with their classification into the five collapsed categories, based on the 10-point left–right scale of party locations adopted from Castles and Mair (1984). New parties which have been added, based on current literature, are marked with an asterisk (*). Election results used are from the annual collation appearing in the *European Journal of Political Research.*

Country	Party name and abbreviation	Left–Right placement	Category
Austria	FMB* – Green/Alternative List	2.5	Moderate left
	SPO – Socialist Party	3.0	Moderate left
	OVP – People's Party	5.8	Centre
	FPO – Freedom Party	6.8	Moderate right
Belgium	KPB/PCB – Communist Party	1.4	Extreme left
	PS – Socialist Party (French)	2.5	Moderate left
	RW – Walloon Rally	2.6	Moderate left
	SP – Socialist Party (Flemish)	2.9	Moderate left
	A/E – Ecology Party	4.5	Centre
	FDF – Francophone Democratic Party	5.6	Centre
	CVP – Christian People's Party	5.8	Centre
	PSC – Christian Socialist Party	6.3	Moderate right
	VU – Flemish People's Party	6.8	Moderate right
	PRL – Liberal Reform Party	7.6	Moderate right
	PVV – Party of Liberty and Progress	7.8	Moderate right
	UDRT/RAD – Democratic Union for the Respect of Labour	9.2	Extreme right
	VB – Flemish Block	9.8	Extreme right

Denmark	VS – Left Socialist Party	0.8	Extreme left
	SF – Socialist People's Party	1.9	Extreme left
	SD – Social Democratic Party	3.8	Moderate left
	RV – Radical Liberal Party	4.8	Centre
	DR* – Justice Party	5.0	Centre
	CD – Centre Democratic Party	5.7	Centre
	KRF – Christian People's Party	6.2	Moderate right
	V – Liberal Party	6.7	Moderate right
	KF – Conservative Party	7.3	Moderate right
	FRP – Progress Party	8.7	Extreme right
Finland	SKDL – Finnish People's Democratic Union	1.8	Extreme left
	VG* – Greens	2.6	Moderate left
	SPD – Social Democratic Party	3.0	Moderate left
	KESK – Centre Party	5.2	Centre
	LKP – Liberal Party	5.6	Centre
	SMP – Rural Party	5.8	Centre
	RKP – Swedish People's Party	6.1	Moderate right
	SKL – Christian League	6.8	Moderate right
	KOK – National Coalition	7.2	Moderate right
Germany	G – Greens	2.8	Moderate left
	SPD – Social Democratic Party	3.3	Moderate left
	FDP – Free Democratic Party	5.1	Centre
	CDU – Christian Democratic Union	6.7	Moderate right
	CSU – Christian Social Union	7.9	Moderate right
Italy	DP – Proletarian Democracy	0.5	Extreme left
	PDUP – Party of Proletarian Unity	0.6	Extreme left
	PCI – Communist Party	1.6	Extreme left
	PR – Radical Party	2.3	Moderate left
	PSI – Socialist Party	3.1	Moderate left
	PRI – Republican Party	4.8	Centre
	DC – Christian Democrats	5.4	Centre
	PSDI – Social Democratic Party	5.4	Centre
	PLI – Liberal Party	5.9	Centre
	MSI – Italian Socialist Movement	9.1	Extreme right
Netherlands	PSP – Pacifist Socialist Party	0.6	Extreme left
	CPN – Communist Party	0.8	Extreme left
	EVP* – Evangelical People's Party	1.0	Extreme left
	PPR – Radical Political Party	1.6	Extreme left
	PvdA – Labour Party	2.6	Moderate left
	D'66 – Democrats '66	4.4	Centre
	CDA – Christian Democratic Appeal	5.7	Centre
	VVD – Liberal Party	7.4	Moderate right
	GPV – Reformed Political League	9.0	Extreme right

	RPF – Reformed Political Federation	9.2	Extreme right
	SGP – Reformed Political Party	9.2	Extreme right
	CP* – Centre Party	9.5	Extreme right
Norway	SV – Left Socialist Party	1.2	Extreme left
	DNA – Labour Party	3.0	Moderate left
	V – Liberal Party	4.0	Centre
	SP – Centre Party	5.8	Centre
	KRF – Christian People's Party	6.1	Moderate right
	H – Conservative Party	7.7	Moderate right
	FP – Progress Party	9.4	Extreme right
Spain	HB – United People	0.5	Extreme left
	UCP – Canary People's Union	0.7	Extreme left
	EE – Basque Left	2.4	Moderate left
	PCE – Communist Party	2.7	Moderate left
	PSOE – Socialist Workers' Party	3.6	Moderate left
	ERC – Republican Left of Catalonia	4.1	Centre
	PSA – Socialist Party of Andalucia	4.5	Centre
	CDS – Democratic and Social Centre	5.0	Centre
	CIU – Convergence and Union	6.6	Moderate right
	PNV – Basque Nationalist Party	6.7	Moderate right
	UCD – Union of the Democratic Centre	7.1	Moderate right
	PAR – Aragonese Regional Party	8.2	Extreme right
	AP – Popular Coalition	8.4	Extreme right
	UN – National Union	9.8	Extreme right
Sweden	VPK – Communist/Left Party	1.2	Extreme left
	SD – Social Democratic Party	2.9	Moderate left
	FP – People's Party	5.5	Centre
	CP – Centre Party	5.9	Centre
	M – Moderate Unity Party	7.7	Moderate right

References

Almond, G.A. (1956) 'Comparative Political Systems', *Journal of Politics*, **18**.

Almond, G.A. and Powell, G.B. Jr (1966) *Comparative Politics: A Developmental Approach*. Boston: Little Brown.

Almond, G.A. and Verba, S. (1963) *The Civic Culture: Political Attitudes and Democracy in Five Nations*. Princeton: Princeton University Press.

Andeweg, R.B. (1982) Dutch voters adrift: on explanations of electoral change 1963–1977. PhD Dissertation, Leyden University.

Barnes, S.H. (1977) *Representation in Italy: Institutionalized Tradition and Electoral Choice*. Chicago: University of Chicago Press.

Bartolini, S. and Mair, P. (1990) 'Policy Competition, Spatial Distance and Electoral Instability', *West European Politics*, **13**.

Bille, L. (1989) 'Denmark: The Oscillating Party System', *West European Politics*, **12**.

Borre, O. (1977) 'Recent Trends in Danish Voting Behavior'. In Cerny, K.H. (ed.) *Scandinavia at the Polls: Recent Political Trends in Denmark, Norway, and Sweden*. Washington: American Enterprise Institute for Public Policy Research.

Borre, O. (1980) 'The Social Bases of Danish Electoral Behaviour'. In Rose, R. (ed.) *Electoral Participation: A Comparative Analysis*. Sage: Beverly Hills.

Borre, O. (1988) 'The Danish General Election of 1987', *Electoral Studies*, **7**.

Budge, I. and Farlie, D. (1983) *Explaining and Predicting Elections*. London: George Allen and Unwin.

Budge, I., Robertson, D. and Hearl, D. (eds) (1987) *Ideology, Strategy and Party Change: Spatial Analyses of Post-War Election Programmes in 19 Democracies*. Cambridge: Cambridge University Press.

Carty, R.K. (1981) *Party and Parish Pump: Electoral Politics in Ireland*. Ontario: Wilfred Laurier University Press.

Castles, F.G. and Mair, P. (1984) 'Left–Right Political Scales: Some "Expert" Judgments', *European Journal of Political Research*, **12**.

Crepaz, M.M.L. (1990) 'The Impact of Party Polarization and Postmaterialism on Voter Turnout: A Comparative Study of 16 Industrial Democracies', *European Journal of Political Research*, **18**.

Daalder, H. (1966) 'The Netherlands: Opposition in a Segmented Society'. In Dahl, R.A. (ed.) *Political Oppositions in Western Democracies*. New Haven: Yale University Press.

Daalder, H. (1971) 'Cabinets and Party Systems in Ten Smaller European Democracies', *Acta Politica*, **6**.

Daalder, H. (1979) 'The Netherlands'. In Henig, S. (ed.) *Political Parties in the European Community*. London: George Allen and Unwin.

Daalder, H. (1984) 'In Search of the Center of European Party Systems', *American Political Science Review*, **78**.

Daalder, H. (1986) 'Changing Procedures and Changing Strategies in Dutch Coalition Building', *Legislative Studies Quarterly*, **11**.

Daalder, H. (1987) 'The Dutch Party System: From Segmentation to Polarization – And Then?' In Daalder, H. (ed.) *Party Systems in Denmark, Austria, Switzerland, The Netherlands, and Belgium*. London: Frances Pinter.

Daalder, H. (1989) 'The Mould of Dutch Politics: Themes for Comparative Inquiry', *West European Politics*, **12**.

Dahl, R.A. (1966) *Political Oppositions in Western Democracies*. New Haven: Yale University Press.

Dahl, R.A. (1970) *After the Revolution*. New Haven: Yale University Press.

Dahl, R.A. (1971) *Polyarchy: Participation and Opposition*. New Haven: Yale University Press.

Dalton, R.J. (1988) *Citizen Politics in Western Democracies: Public Opinion and Political Parties in the United States, Great Britain, West Germany, and France*. Chatham: Chatham House.

Damgaard, E. (1969) 'The Parliamentary Basis of Danish Governments: The Patterns of Coalition Formation', *Scandinavian Political Studies*, **4**.

Damgaard, E. (1973) 'Party Coalitions in Danish Law-Making 1953–70', *European Journal of Political Research*, **1**.

Damgaard, E. and Rusk, J.G. (1976) 'Cleavage Structures and Representational Linkages: A Longitudinal Analysis of Danish Legislative Behaviour'. In Budge, I., Crewe, I. and Farlie, D. (eds) *Party Identification and Beyond: Representations of Voting and Party Competition*. London: John Wiley and Sons.

de Swaan, A. (1973) *Coalition Theories and Cabinet Formations: A Study of Formal Theories of Coalition Formation Applied to Nine European Parliaments After 1918*. San Francisco: Jossey-Bass.

de Swaan, A. (1982) 'The Netherlands: Coalitions in a Segmented Polity'. In Browne, E.C. and Dreijmanis, J. (eds) *Government Coalitions in Western Democracies*. New York: Longman.

Dittrich, K. (1987) 'The Netherlands 1946–1981'. In Budge, I., Robertson, D. and Hearl, D. (eds) *Ideology, Strategy and Party Change: Spatial Analyses of Post-War Election Programmes in 19 Democracies.* Cambridge: Cambridge University Press.

Dodd, L.C. (1974) 'Party Coalitions in Multiparty Parliaments: A Game-Theoretic Analysis', *American Political Science Review,* **68.**

Dodd, L.C. (1976) *Coalitions in Parliamentary Government.* Princeton: Princeton University Press.

Downs, A. (1957) *An Economic Theory of Democracy.* New York: Harper and Row.

Duverger, M. (1959) *Political Parties: Their Organization and Activity in the Modern State.* New York: John Wiley and Sons.

Einhorn, E.S. and Logue, J. (1988) 'Continuity and Change in the Scandinavian Party Systems'. In Wolinetz, S.B. (ed.) *Parties and Party Systems in Liberal Democracies.* London: Routledge.

Elder, N., Thomas, A.H. and Arter, D. (1982) *The Consensual Democracies? The Government and Politics of the Scandinavian States.* Oxford: Martin Robertson.

Elklit, J. (1993) 'Simpler Than its Reputation: The Electoral System in Denmark Since 1920', *Electoral Studies,* **12.**

Elklit, J., Riis, O. and Tonsgaard, O. (1972) 'Local Voting Studies of Total Electorates: The Danish General Election of 1971', *Scandinavian Political Studies,* **7.**

Ersson, S. and Lane, J.-E. (1982) 'Democratic Party Systems in Europe: Dimensions, Change and Stability', *Scandinavian Political Studies,* **5.**

Farneti, P. (1985) *The Italian Party System 1945–1980.* London: Frances Pinter.

Fitzmaurice, J. (1981) *Politics in Denmark.* London: C. Hurst and Co.

Gallagher, M. (1981) 'Societal Change and Party Adaptation in the Republic of Ireland, 1960–1981', *European Journal of Political Research,* **9.**

Galli, G. (1966) *Il Bipartitismo Imperfetto.* Bologna: Il Mulino.

Galli, G. (1975) *Dal Bipartitismo Imperfetto alla Possibile Alternativa.* Bologna: Il Mulino.

Gladdish, K. (1983) 'The 1982 Netherlands Election', *West European Politics,* **6.**

Hazan, R.Y. (1994) 'Partiti di Centro e Partiti Centrali: Una Chiarificazione Concettuale', *Rivista Italiana di Scienza Politica,* **24.**

Holmstedt, M. and Schou, T.-L. (1987) 'Sweden and Denmark: Election Programmes in the Scandinavian Setting'. In Budge, I., Robertson, D. and Hearl, D. (eds) *Ideology, Strategy and Party Change: Spatial Analyses of Post-War Election Programmes in 19 Democracies.* Cambridge: Cambridge University Press.

Ieraci, G. (1992) 'Centre Parties and Anti-System Oppositions in Polarised Systems', *West European Politics,* **15.**

Inglehart, R. and Klingemann, H.D. (1976) 'Party Identification, Ideological Preference and the Left–Right Dimension Among Western Mass Publics'. In Budge, I., Crewe, I. and Farlie, D. (eds) *Party Identification and Beyond: Representation of Voting and Party Competition.* New York: John Wiley and Sons.

Irving, R.E.M. (1979) *The Christian Democratic Parties of Western Europe.* London: George Allen and Unwin.

Irwin, G.A. (1980) 'Patterns of Voting Behaviour in The Netherlands'. In Griffiths, R.T. (ed.) *The Economy and Politics of The Netherlands Since 1945.* The Hague: Martinus Nijhoff.

Irwin, G.A. and van Holsteyn, J.J.M. (1989a) 'Towards a More Open Model of Competition', *West European Politics,* **12**.

Irwin, G.A. and van Holsteyn, J.J.M. (1989b) 'Decline of the Structured Model of Electoral Competition', *West European Politics,* **12**.

Janda, K. (1975) 'A Worldwide Study of Political Parties'. In Mittman, B. and Borman, L. (eds) *Personalized Data Base Systems.* New York: John Wiley and Sons.

Jarlov, C. and Kristensen, O.P. (1978) 'Electoral Mobility and Social Change in Denmark', *Scandinavian Political Studies,* **1**.

Johansen, L.N. (1982) 'Denmark'. In Hand, G., George, G. and Sasse, C. (eds) *European Electoral Systems Handbook.* London: Butterworths.

Keman, H. (1994) 'The Search for the Center: Pivot Parties in West European Party Systems', *West European Politics,* **17**.

Kendall, M.G. and Stuart, A. (1950) 'The Law of the Cubic Proportion in Election Results', *British Journal of Sociology,* **1**.

Lane, J.-E. and Ersson, S. (1987) 'Multipartism'. In Holler, M.J. (ed.) *The Logic of Multiparty Systems.* Dordrecht: Martinus Nijhoff.

Laponce, J.A. (1970) 'Note on the Use of the Left–Right Dimension', *Comparative Political Studies,* **2**.

Laponce, J.A. (1981) *Left and Right: The Topography of Political Perceptions.* Toronto: University of Toronto Press.

Laver, M. (1974) 'Dynamic Factors in Government Coalition Formation', *European Journal of Political Research,* **2**.

Laver, M.J. and Budge, I. (eds) (1992) *Party Policy and Government Coalitions.* New York: St Martin's.

Lijphart, A. (1968) *The Politics of Accommodation: Pluralism and Democracy in The Netherlands.* Berkeley: University of California Press.

Lijphart, A. (1974) 'Consociational Democracy'. In McRae, K.D. (ed.) *Consociational Democracy: Political Accommodation in Segmented Societies.* Toronto: McClelland and Stewart.

Lijphart, A. (1975) *The Politics of Accommodation: Pluralism and Democracy in The Netherlands,* 2nd edition. Berkeley: University of California Press.

Lijphart, A. (1977) *Democracy in Plural Societies: A Comparative Exploration.* New Haven: Yale University Press.

Lijphart, A. (1982) 'The Relative Salience of the Socio-Economic and Religious Issue Dimensions: Coalition Formations in Ten Western Democracies, 1919–1979', *European Journal of Political Research*, **10**.

Lijphart, A. (1984) 'Measures of Cabinet Durability: A Conceptual and Empirical Analysis', *Comparative Political Studies*, **17**.

Lipset, S.M. (1959) *Political Man.* Garden City: Doubleday.

Lipset, S.M. and Rokkan, S. (eds) (1967) *Party Systems and Voter Alignments: Cross-national Perspectives.* New York: Free Press.

Marradi, A. (1982) 'Italy: From "Centrism" to Crisis of the Center–Left Coalitions'. In Browne, E.C. and Dreijmanis, J. (eds) *Government Coalitions in Western Democracies.* New York: Longman.

Mayer, L.C. (1989) *Redefining Comparative Politics: Promise Versus Performance.* London: Sage.

Midlarsky, M.I. (1984) 'Political Stability of Two-Party and Multiparty Systems: Probabilistic Bases for the Comparison of Party Systems', *American Political Science Review*, **78**.

Miller, K.E. (1964) 'The Danish Electoral System', *Parliamentary Affairs*, **18**.

Nannestad, P. (1989) *Reactive Voting in Danish General Elections 1971–1979.* Aarhus: Aarhus University Press.

Neumann, S. (ed.) (1956) *Modern Political Parties: Approaches to Comparative Politics.* Chicago: University of Chicago Press.

Nielsen, H.J. (1976) 'The Uncivic Culture: Attitudes Toward the Political System in Denmark, and Vote for the Progress Party 1973–1975', *Scandinavian Political Studies*, **11**.

Nielsen, K. and Pedersen, O.K. (1989) 'Is Small Still Flexible? – An Evaluation of Recent Trends in Danish Politics', *Scandinavian Political Studies*, **12**.

Pasquino, G. (1986) 'Modernity and Reformers: The PSI Between Political Entrepreneurs and Gamblers', *West European Politics*, **9**.

Pedersen, M.N. (1966) 'Preferential Voting in Denmark: The Voters' Influence on the Election of Folketing Candidates', *Scandinavian Political Studies*, **1**.

Pedersen, M.N. (1967) 'Consensus and Conflict in the Danish Folketing 1945–65', *Scandinavian Political Studies*, **2**.

Pedersen, M.N. (1979) 'The Dynamics of European Party Systems: Changing Patterns of Electoral Volatility', *European Journal of Political Research*, **7**.

Pedersen, M.N. (1987) 'The Danish "Working Multiparty System": Breakdown or Adaptation?' In Daalder, H. (ed.) *Party Systems in Denmark, Austria, Switzerland, The Netherlands, and Belgium.* London: Frances Pinter.

Pedersen, M.N., Damgaard, E. and Olsen, P.N. (1971) 'Party Distances in the Danish Folketing 1945–1968', *Scandinavian Political Studies*, **6**.

Powell, G.B. Jr (1981) 'Party Systems and Political System Performance: Voting Participation, Government Stability and Mass Violence in Contemporary Democracies', *American Political Science Review*, **75**.

Powell, G.B. Jr (1982) *Contemporary Democracies: Participation, Stability, and Violence.* Cambridge: Harvard University Press.

Powell, G.B. Jr (1986) 'Extreme Parties and Political Turmoil: Two Puzzles', *American Journal of Political Science*, **30**.

Powell, G.B. Jr (1987) 'The Competitive Consequences of Polarized Pluralism'. In Holler, M.J. (ed.) *The Logic of Multiparty Systems.* Dordrecht: Martinus Nijhoff.

Przeworski, A. and Teune, H. (1970) *The Logic of Comparative Social Inquiry.* New York: John Wiley and Sons.

Rae, D.W. (1967) *The Political Consequences of Electoral Laws.* New Haven: Yale University Press.

Rémy, D. (1975) 'The Pivotal Party: Definitions and Measurement', *European Journal of Political Research*, **3**.

Rokkan, S. (1977) 'Towards A Generalized Concept of *Verzuiling*', *Political Studies*, **25**.

Rose, R. and McAllister, I. (1986) *Voters Begin to Choose: From Closed-Class to Open Elections in Britain.* London: Sage.

Rusk, J.G. and Borre, O. (1974) 'The Changing Party Space in Danish Voter Perceptions, 1971–1973', *European Journal of Political Research*, **2**.

Rustow, D.A. (1956) 'Scandinavia: Working Multiparty Systems'. In Neumann, S. (ed.) *Modern Political Parties: Approaches to Comparative Politics.* Chicago: University of Chicago Press.

Sanders, D. and Herman, V. (1977) 'The Stability and Survival of Governments in Western Democracies', *Acta Politica*, **12**.

Sani, G. and Sartori, G. (1983) 'Polarization, Fragmentation and Competition in Western Democracies'. In Daalder, H. and Mair, P. (eds) *Western European Party Systems: Continuity and Change.* London: Sage.

Sartori, G. (1966) 'European Political Parties: The Case of Polarized Pluralism'. In LaPalombara, J. and Weiner, M. (eds) *Political Parties and Political Development.* Princeton: Princeton University Press.

Sartori, G. (1976) *Parties and Party Systems: A Framework for Analysis.* Cambridge: Cambridge University Press.

Scully, T.R. (1992) *Rethinking the Center: Party Politics in Nineteenth- and Twentieth-Century Chile.* Stanford: Stanford University Press.

Seliger, M. (1976) *Ideology and Politics.* London: George Allen and Unwin.

Sigelman, L. and Yough, S.N. (1978) 'Left–Right Polarization in National Party Systems: A Cross-National Analysis', *Comparative Political Studies*, **11**.

Starzinger, V.E. (1965) *Middlingness: Juste Milieu Political Theory in France and England, 1815–48.* Charlottesville: University Press of Virginia.

Stokes, D.E. (1963) 'Spatial Models of Party Competition', *American Political Science Review*, **57**.

Tarrow, S. (1977) 'The Italian Party System Between Crisis and Transition', *American Journal of Political Science*, **21**.

Taylor, M. and Herman, V.M. (1971) 'Party Systems and Government Stability', *American Political Science Review*, **65**.

Taylor, M. and Laver, M. (1973) 'Government Coalitions in Western Europe', *European Journal of Political Research*, **1**.

Thomas, J.C. (1982) 'Ideological Change in Comparative Labor Parties: A Test of Downsian Theory', *Comparative Political Studies*, **15**.

van der Eijk, C. and Niemöller, B. (1983) *Electoral Change in the Netherlands: Empirical Results and Methods of Measurement.* Amsterdam: CT Press.

van der Eijk, C. and Niemöller, B. (1985) 'The Netherlands'. In Crewe, I. and Denver, D. (eds) *Electoral Change in Western Democracies: Patterns and Sources of Electoral Volatility.* London: Croom Helm.

van Loenen, G. (1990) 'Weimar or Byzantium: Two Opposing Approaches to the Italian Party System', *European Journal of Political Research*, **18**.

van Mierlo, H.J.G.A. (1986) 'Depillarisation and the Decline of Consociationalism in The Netherlands: 1970–85', *West European Politics*, **9**.

van Roozendaal, P. (1990) 'Centre Parties and Coalition Cabinet Formations: A Game Theoretic Approach', *European Journal of Political Research*, **18**.

Wolinetz, S.B. (1974) Party re-alignment in The Netherlands. PhD Dissertation, Yale University.

Wolinetz, S.B. (1990) 'The Dutch Election of 1989: Return to the Centre-Left', *West European Politics*, **13**.

Worre, T. (1980) 'Class Parties and Class Voting in the Scandinavian Countries', *Scandinavian Political Studies*, **3**.

Index